Raven Ruthe

⋈

A Bleary-Eyed
Stranger

How faith, love and God
healed my addict daughter

Mereo Books

2nd Floor, 6-8 Dyer Street, Cirencester, Gloucestershire, GL7 2PF
An imprint of Memoirs Books. www.mereobooks.com
and www.memoirsbooks.co.uk

Title of Book: A Bleary-Eyed Stranger
ISBN: 978-1-86151-856-9

First published in Great Britain in 2021
by Mereo Books, an imprint of Memoirs Books.

Copyright ©2021

Raven Ruthe has asserted her right under the Copyright Designs and Patents Act 1988
to be identified as the author of this work.

A CIP catalogue record for this book is available from the British Library.
This book is sold subject to the condition that it shall not by way of trade or otherwise
be lent, resold, hired out or otherwise circulated without the publisher's prior consent
in any form of binding or cover, other than that in which it is published and without a
similar condition, including this condition being imposed on the subsequent purchaser.

The address for Memoirs Books can be found at www.mereobooks.com

Mereo Books Ltd. Reg. No. 12157152

Typeset in 11/15pt Century Schoolbook
by Wiltshire Associates.
Printed and bound in Great Britain

"For we walk by faith, not by sight"

(Second Corinthians)

Author's Note

Anonymity is the spiritual foundation of the 12-Step Program for recovery from addiction. Accordingly all names and identifying details have been changed to protect the privacy of individuals. Any resemblance to some actual persons or events other than my daughter is coincidental.

Dedication

"A Bleary-Eyed Stranger, how faith, love and God healed my daughter," is dedicated to all families with loved ones struggling with addiction.

To my daughter who struggled with addiction and is now in recovery. I am grateful we are on this journey together. You are loved and cherished. Your strength and willingness to heal yourself inspires me every day.

To my cherished father, who taught me the meaning of unconditional love, and how faith and strength comes from one's relationship with God; and to Lee, spiritual sister and confidante, thank-you for always being there for me.

Introduction

Six weeks ago as I write this, on March 11, 2020, I pulled the covers over my head and began coping with the pandemic. Together, my daughter Jess and I followed the suggestions and dictates of the quarantine—stay at home, order take-out. We watched television and went to online meetings—she to Alcoholics Anonymous, me to Al-Anon, a fellowship and spiritual program based on the 12 Steps of Alcoholics Anonymous.

Before March 11, I had been facilitating training in nursing homes for a local hospice and providing mental health services in both my group and private practice. When the pandemic hit, my daughter and I lost our jobs. I got into bed, pulled the covers over my head, and let my daughter take care of things in the house. With no income and an ongoing concern about the virus, Jess took on a stronger role with household chores. Now the roles were reversed—she was taking care of me in the same way I had been taking care of her for the past three years, as I gratefully watched her addiction go into remission. I, on the other hand, got sick when a gastrointestinal issue flared, something I hadn't had since I was thirty-one years old.

Watching my daughter's struggle with opioid addiction over the years, I sometimes wrote about it, but I often abandoned the writing project, thinking I would never publish an account of such a personal journey. I am a private person, a psychotherapist who helps people with trauma and addiction. Slowly, I emerged from the grief and loss of my job and income, and the isolation of self-quarantine, and began writing my story. The opioid epidemic is still going on. Family members continue to deal with the trauma associated with the pandemic and with their loved one's addiction, just as I have. I am writing to share my experience, strength and hope, and how faith in God strengthened Jess and I as we walked together through her addiction back to recovery.

Foreword

by Jess

There is nothing funny about addiction. Addiction in any form, be it gambling, drug and alcohol or sex addiction, is a brutal conflict fought inside the self. The universe within is the arena for this fight, and no one but the person going through it can accurately appreciate it in its entirety. At my lowest point, I wouldn't have wished addiction on my worst enemy. If you can avoid it in some way, more power to you.

I am a true addict, swimming into the deep end with both arms and legs. There is no question that I am an addict. By the end of my addiction, the greatest battles I went through—how much I used or when or where I used—made zero headway in beating my addiction. Any plans I made about what day I would stop using and how I would go about stopping were useless. Though these statements may sound repetitive, they represent the big picture of how difficult it is to stop using drugs, and the absolute futility of attempting to stop using without interventions. In the end, I would have liked to take an easier, softer way to recovery. But that's a fantasy. In my heart, I know there is no such thing. In other words, once an addict, always an addict. Of course, that's not the totality of who I am, but I have to remind myself every day that I am an addict so I don't delude myself into thinking I can do anything recreationally, like have a drink or smoke a joint. Can't happen!

Over the past ten years I have learned that the only way out is *through*, meaning I had to learn to walk through the darkest times alone. The support of my mother and father was always there, but this was my journey and my private hell. I had to figure it out alone. There was nothing they could do to stop me from using drugs. Eventually, I discovered that my greatest support and ally was my higher power. I am not good at surrendering or leaning on anything. I have a strong will—my mother tells me I always have had. Gradually, I had to surrender my will completely to a higher power, begging on my knees for help. In the end, my higher power, God, allowed me to find a better way of life. My life now is infinitely better than the life I was living out on the streets in Kensington,

Philadelphia. My faith is strong knowing God "restored me to sanity."

2012: Dopesick in Tokyo

In 2012, before I knew anything about what physical addiction truly was and while I was abusing opioids and benzodiazepines, I decided to embark on a three-week trip to Japan, mainly the Nakameguro section of Tokyo. I was staying with a college friend who was from Tokyo. We had met in college in my twenties, but I had not seen him since then. When I went to Tokyo I was in my early thirties and deep into an opioid addiction I knew little about, or the consequences it would bring. I was in denial, thinking it was something I could handle, and I could stop using at any time if I chose to do so. Addiction takes hold fast and choice disappears in a flash. I didn't know my brain had been hijacked and that I was lying to myself. I told myself I was in control. No one in my family knew I was struggling with addiction. *I* didn't even know I was struggling with addiction!

The first night in Tokyo, my Japanese friend was nice enough to take me out to dinner. At first I was joined just by his girlfriend, now his wife, and another male friend of his. They both spoke little English but I still had a great time trying to communicate with them. Their job was to entertain me until my college friend was finished with work.

Once he arrived, I learned the true nature of what it means to be a young employee in Tokyo. Having just taken a new job, my friend arrived after 11 pm. For the Japanese, the work day doesn't end at five o'clock. The expectation is that after the close of the work day, an employee is more or less required to go out for drinks with his coworkers. Since my friend was the newest employee in the company he had to stay late and participate in after-work social events. Arriving at eleven o'clock at night for dinner with other friends was not unusual. And this wasn't a once-a-week thing for him, this was every night of the week. Being the newest and youngest member in the company he was required to be the first one at work in the morning. His first job was to make coffee for the entire office.

When I had called him from the States and arranged to go to Tokyo, he was still looking for work. We both thought we would have time to spend together in Tokyo, but by the time I got there he had taken the new job and things had changed drastically for him, and for me. I was already a drug addict, believing the fantasy that I could just stop using opioids at any time, no problem. Instead,

I began to go through physical withdrawal from opioids and benzodiazepines. My friend was working, unable to give me the support I needed through a medically supervised detox, but now that wouldn't be possible—and I didn't even know I was an addict.

The first night I was there in Tokyo and before I started withdrawing was a blast. We all drank until the sun came up, and for me this was twelve hours or more behind the actual time I was on with jet lag, so my night was just getting started. For him it was quite the opposite. When the sun rose and we went back to his apartment to settle in, he got in the shower, got dressed, and left for work. The last thing he told me was to stay up all day so I could get on a normal schedule for the next three weeks I would spend there with him. Little did I know what was brewing inside my body in terms of my addiction to opioids, something I thought I could beat if I just tried hard enough.

I fell asleep in the early hours of the morning in his one-room studio apartment, with no idea of what was in store for me. Six hours later, I awoke in the throes of a flu-like sickness. Until that nightmare moment in Tokyo, I was unable to truly understand withdrawal. To this day, I am haunted by nighttime dreams of flying overseas only to go into withdrawal. I will spare you the graphic details, but let me say that along with a raging sickness inside your body, the mind turns to despair and hopelessness. NO ONE has truly experienced hopelessness unless they have been though addiction and survived. I understand very bad depression can be similar, but it goes without the raging, violent physical sickness of throwing up, aches, pains, chills, and fever inside your body.

I will spare you the full details of my trip, but long story short, I ended up in the Tokyo hospital, not once but twice, begging for opioids, telling them that in my country they were routinely given by doctors to patients in this kind of situation. I was desperate and sick. My poor college friend translating for me asked if I was asking for opioids because I wanted them, or because I needed them. He must have understood on some level what was going on. In the end, I changed my flight and just short of two weeks after arriving in Tokyo, I was back in the USA.

Fall 2012

After not learning my lesson in Tokyo, I quickly got back in touch with my friends who used drugs and started taking pills again. It was mostly Xanax, a benzodiazepine generally prescribed for anxiety, and opioids. I was drinking, smoking pot, snorting coke, and taking acid (LSD), a hallucinogenic drug, as well as eating psychedelic mushrooms and anything else I could get my hands on other than heroin to get me out of myself. It wasn't till I ended up at a recovery house in Kensington, where heroin is sold openly on the street corners, that I started using this very highly addictive drug.

But I don't want to focus on war stories. We all have them and at the heart of the addiction they are similar—living on the streets. I was doing things I would never have done had I not been an addict. This is a disease of give me just one more drug, one more time, one more bag, anything so I don't have to face not using and begin the hard process of withdrawal. But it never ends. A disease is defined as progressive and deadly, and addiction is just that. It gets progressively worse, and eventually kills you if you don't stop. It is the number one killer of young people in the disease category. Think about that for a second. More people under the age of forty die from the disease of addiction than die in car accidents, from suicide, or any other horrible way to die you can think of. Before the pandemic, the opioid crisis was all anyone could talk about—it was big news every day of the week. Now I don't hear much.

I first started taking opioids after a sports injury. It

was chronic and always nagging, a dull pain. After years of only taking them sporadically, I eventually hooked up with a friend who was already addicted to them. He showed me where to get them, what to say to doctors, what pharmacies would fill the scripts and how to avoid withdrawal—in other words, keep using. In Tokyo, I finally understood what withdrawal was all about, and how dangerous it is without medical help. Being in another country and not having access to opioids and a medical detox was the only way I was ever able to experience the pain of withdrawal, and it was serious, awful pain.

At the end of a long lifetime run, and desperately needing help, I finally asked my father, a man who struggled with addiction and has had forty years in recovery, to step in and help me. Once my mom knew I was using drugs and before my insurance kicked in so I could go to a recovery house, she wouldn't let me come home. My parents were in agreement: I couldn't use drugs and be part of the family in the same way. No more family dinners until I got myself together, and that would take four more years after I made a decision to go on methadone, a medication used to treat opioid abuse disorder. My parents were on the same page to help me get better but I had to figure it out.

As I waited for the insurance to take effect, unable to

go home, the best plan was to use an empty room next to my dad's office and sleep there. This would be my second experience with cold turkey withdrawal, just as bad as when I was in Tokyo. I begged to anyone who would listen to help me, but if I had known then what I know now, I would have immediately gone to a methadone clinic. Throughout the years struggling with addiction and not knowing what to do next, I tried Suboxone, a prescription medicine used to treat addiction. For me it didn't work. I know it works for other people; everybody is different. Different medications like methadone and Suboxone work according to the person's willingness and readiness for recovery.

To sum it all up, I eventually got sober during an especially dangerous relapse, when I abruptly stopped taking opioids and benzodiazepines and a vicious withdrawal set in. An abrupt withdrawal can actually kill a person. I ended up in a mental institution, wearing a diaper, totally shot out. After a month of that hard and scary experience where I couldn't put a coherent thought together, I discharged myself. I left the hospital without shoes, got on the subway and headed home. After that I took methadone treatment seriously and got sober.

Let me tell you that sober life has incrementally gotten more and more amazing. The first year was brutal, with constant fantasies about using drugs. Then after a year or two, the cravings for drugs started to subside. By year four I was flying happy pretty much every day, making music again, working, and rarely thinking about picking up one day at a time. Our family is back together. I am included in all events with my dad and his wife and his other children, my brothers and sisters. Life at home with Mom is working out well. My disease is in remission. I am getting better.

My best advice is this: at the beginning of my recovery, I relied heavily on a program. I chose Alcoholics Anonymous. It's a spiritual program that teaches the importance of surrendering to God – not my will but God's will – and practicing meditation and contemplation on God and daily prayer. You can choose any 12-step program, but try something, anything, that feels right and is helpful, because you can't do recovery on your own. At first it will feel strange, like wearing a wet pair of pants, but eventually you will feel right at home. And definitely start practicing the steps of the 12-step program, especially the first one: "We admitted we were powerless over alcohol and that our lives had become unmanageable."

Steps Two and Three are about developing a relationship with a God of your understanding. That comes later, at least it did for me. Get a sponsor, and don't wait until you're ready, just make a personal inventory of what you want to accomplish, who you are, and what you have been through, and tell your secrets to someone in the 12-Step program, or a clergy person. Tell someone who won't judge you and who will help you. You have nothing to lose by trying. And share as much as you feel comfortable sharing with others. Don't forget to reach out for help.

The 12 Steps is a program of service and people get better by helping others as well as asking for help. I have found helping people benefits me more than anything else I do. The other piece of advice I have is do not fantasize about using drugs. Those thoughts have to be pushed away immediately. Thoughts become ideas, and then we are speaking them aloud and calling the dealer. Words become actions. Stop with the fantasy, it is dangerous. And third, possibly the hardest is make new friends. You have zero chance of getting sober if you still spend time with people who are using drugs. I have told people from my drug-using days, people that I care deeply about, that I won't be seeing them until they are ready to get sober as well.

To anyone struggling with addiction, my heart goes out to you, it really does. Only a true addict can come close to understanding another addict. That's why Alcoholics Anonymous (AA) and Narcotics Anonymous (NA) are successful at helping others through their struggle. The idea that you can smoke a joint one time, drink a drink socially on weekends could end up getting you killed. I never saw so many people die before I entered the rooms of AA. Young people drop dead from an overdose on a weekly basis, and that is not a joke. It's a quick way to kill yourself, no matter how careful you are. Statements like "I only snort it," or "just one more bag," are deadly. I had a friend tell me she could never overdose from heroin and that people who say it's possible are liars. That person ended up dead the following year from taking one bag of dope because she had no tolerance. She picked up a needle, shot heroin, and died.

I am writing this foreword to briefly tell you my experience so it can help you understand a bit more about what goes on for your loved one. People say they don't want to use again, and then they relapse. Someone looking in from the outside may see that as a weak will, but that is not true. It is totally a response to a hijacked, addicted brain. The strength of one's will power disappears. Hopefully this book and my foreword will give some insight and help you understand what goes on in the addict brain, perhaps increasing empathy and compassion for someone like me, a regular person, and a struggling addict.

Chapter 1

Sunlight streams in through the bay windows. It's Sunday morning, May 20th 2013, not a cloud in the sky. I'm lazing about, catching up on paperwork, paying bills and making a to-do list when the cellphone beeps. A text message from Jim, my ex-husband says: "Jess is high as a kite driving to Boston. She called from the turnpike. She has the dog, stereo, her clothes. All her belongings packed in the car. She can't see out the back window." The text continued with words that still made no sense: "I told her to pull into a rest stop and put her stuff in the trunk so she can see out the back window. I'd meet her there at the rest stop." I read the message again and again, unable to make sense out of any of it.

"She's not coming home, Raven," Jim continued. "She told me not to come to the rest stop, not to follow her. She doesn't trust us. We'll put her in a recovery house or hospital, and she knows it."

"What are you talking about? Who are you talking about?" I text in response, certain the man I've known since he was eighteen years old, the father of my daughter, sent these texts to the wrong person. He couldn't possibly be talking about our daughter? Our Jess, my Jess, didn't use drugs or drink alcohol!

The next few days were a blur of rising panic. All I knew was that my daughter—my only child, the child I'd raised as a single mother while her father struggled with his own addiction—was driving high somewhere between Philadelphia and Boston. The thought of Jess driving on the New Jersey Turnpike in that state of mind, endangering other people's lives and her own, competed with my own mother's voice: "Don't tell anyone what's going on. Don't air your dirty laundry in public."

Chapter 2

"I'd like to make a reservation." Packing a suitcase, I leave the house where Jess and I live. My ex-husband tells me Jess will come home high, out of control. Heart pounding, I call the hotel and the veterinarian's office to board our other dog.

"My dog has been there before. I'd like to board him for a few days. Is there room?"

"Yes, there is room. When will you be dropping him off?"

"I can bring him right now," I say to the scheduler. I grab the car keys and lockup the house, hoping Jess won't come home. With one dog safe and one less thing to worry about, I drive to the vet, drop the dog off, and go back to the house. I send a text message to Jim: "I dropped the dog off at the vet. I'm home again. Staying here is not an option. I made a reservation at the Extended Stay near the Mall. I hope Jess and the dog Bruce are safe. Have you heard from Jess?"

"No I haven't heard from her. You're making the right decision. Get out of the house. You don't know what condition Jess will be in, she's probably high or crashing and looking for a place to sleep. She will insist on coming home to sleep in her room. You will have a hard time saying no. Don't worry about Bruce. He is Jess's dog. She will take care of Bruce. Text me if you hear anything."

"I'm leaving now and locking up the house. I worry about Bruce. Jess is high and out of it. She could forget about Bruce and leave him at the rest stop. She could forget she's taking care of her dog." Closing my eyes, I pick up the phone and call Jess, and leave her a message: "Don't come home. You can't stay here. When you're high, you are not welcome at the house or in the neighborhood. Go to the emergency room hospital. If you come here you cannot come inside or sleep on the back porch. Get help for yourself. Daddy and I will help you but not while you are high. Go to a hospital, crisis center, or emergency center. Take care of yourself. Take care of Bruce."

"Don't worry, Mom. I won't come home to your precious house," Jess's voice message says. "I won't let the neighbors know your daughter is a drug addict failure. I won't embarrass you. Of course I'll take care of Bruce. I know you've been taking care of Bruce but I love him too. I'm not coming home. If I do come home you will try and trap me." She is afraid that we are going to call the police and have her arrested.

We call the police.

"We can't arrest someone who has not done anything wrong," The precinct police officer says.

"She's driving high! If you arrest her, you might be saving her life and someone else's life too." I plead with the police officer on the phone, not knowing where Jess is or how the police would find her. She hasn't broken the law. I hang up the phone and back out of the driveway onto the street.

Jess pulls into the driveway. She is home.

The black Subaru is packed to the roof: stereo equipment, shoes, winter and summer clothes. The car is overflowing with empty junk food bags, spilled soda bottles, puddles on the car floor. Bruce whines, hopping from one paw to the other on the front seat of the car.

"Give me the dog," I say, reaching in the open driver's side window, grabbing the car keys. They fall out of the ignition and onto the mat on the car floor. A hot flash of pain, my breast is jammed against the steering wheel. Jess backs out of the garage, tire wheels spinning, gravel shooting out from the undercarriage of the car. She accelerates the Subaru, roars down the street, and disappears in a cloud of dust.

Jess's father leaves a message on her phone:

"Jess. Come home. We are trying to help you. We have names of rehabs and recovery houses. Go to the hospital emergency room. You need help! Do something to help yourself."

"I will meet you at your house," Jim texts to me. "I have a plan, an intervention. I will reason with her. Jess will listen to me."

A few hours later, Jess returns to the house. She drives into the driveway and gets out of the car. A trapped rabbit, she knows something is up. She jumps back into the car, guns the engine and races across the neighbor's manicured lawn.

Later that evening, at the Extended Stay Hotel, I take the Bible out of the drawer and read a verse on faith. "Now faith is the assurance of things hoped for the conviction of things not seen." I flip through television channels, too wired to sleep. I close the Bible and pray. "Dear God, take care of my daughter Jess. Keep her safe in your love, your healing light away from darkness. Help Jess make the right decision and be guided by your wisdom. Strengthen my faith, keep me strong."

For three nights I stay at the hotel, reading the Bible and praying things will quiet down. I pray that Jess will come to her senses and stop using drugs, and that the house will not be trashed when I return home.

Chapter 3

Jess is a smart, reasonable person. She knows her father is a recovering addict and alcoholic with three decades of recovery. Health classes taught her about addiction. She knew she was at a higher risk than others who did not have addiction in their family history. We often talked about never using drugs or drinking alcohol in fear of the genetic component of addiction taking hold.

"You don't have to worry about me, Mom," Jess reassured me, while denying smoking pot as a teenager while sitting in her room with friends after school; a strange smell emanating from down the hall.

"What's that burning smell?"

"It's nothing, Mom," she said, and I believed her. Perhaps my own denial delayed her recovery. I didn't want to know. Still I ask, what happened? At the time, I believed addiction could be controlled by willpower, or the love of a parent for a child so strong that the child would do nothing wrong. At the time, when I was forty-six years old and Jess was thirteen, I did not know that addiction is a disease that when left untreated could get worse. Those were the days when I wore a T-shirt that said, "Just Do It! Pull yourself up by your bootstraps." In other words, keep moving forward, don't look back. If you are using drugs, you can stop from sheer willpower.

During my marriage, I often asked myself why Jim could not stop drinking or using drugs. But addiction profoundly changes the brain cells, creating new brain pathways, a new and different set of signals that increase physical and mental cravings, telling the brain to use more drugs and drink more alcohol. "Imagine fertilizing weeds with Miracle Grow. The weeds will spread unchecked across the lawn. The opiate receptor sites in the brain grow in the same way," I tell my clients and my daughter, "and people lose control quickly."

The next few weeks are a blur. Jim and I search for

rehabs and recovery houses, only to discover that they don't take our daughter's insurance. I call Jess, hoping she will pick up the phone.

"Daddy and I have been trying to get you into recovery houses but you need to change your insurance. Go to a crisis center. They will help you get into a hospital. The social worker will apply for Medicaid, your new insurance," I say, leaving her a message.

At two o'clock in the morning, Jess returns the call.

"I'm at the WAWA and I need money."

"Come home. Bring the car home and bring the dog home."

"I need food and money!" she shouts.

"Give me Bruce. He's my dog too!" I shout back over the phone, grabbing my jacket. "Which WAWA? Where are you?"

"You know which WAWA," Jess says, slurring her words.

"Stay there. I'll be over in fifteen minutes." *Can I get Jess to reason with me so I can get the dog?*

Jess slams down the phone.

"Give me Bruce," I say, meeting up with her. I speak softly, trying not to draw attention to the 2 am WAWA crowd. I reach through the open window of the car for the keys. Jess closes the window on my arm. The dog whimpers, people stare.

"You are hurting my arm," I say through clenched teeth. "Please give me the dog," I plead, trying a different approach. Has Jess forgotten that I am her mother and that I love her, raised her, nurtured her, drove her to school? Her friends were always welcome at the house, enjoying sleepovers on weekends, parties, and play dates.

A stream of white cigarette smoke streams out of the Subaru window. My daughter, a bleary, red-eyed, paranoid stranger, is blowing it out the window into my face.

"My arm is caught. Roll down the friggin' window!" Jess inches the window down. I pull out my arm.

"Give me the dog!" I shout. Bruce whimpers.

"Give me Bruce," I demand. "He wants to come with me, please," I plead, lowering my voice, hoping Jess will hear me and respond to reason. But my daughter is too far gone. I reach back into the car for the keys; gray smoke streams out the window of the Subaru, blinding us both.

"Get out of the car right now. It's my car. I pay the bills on the car. Damn it Jess! Get out of the car and give me Bruce!" Jess rolls up the window. My arm is caught again and crushed. Bruce is whimpering to reach me.

"Get your arm out of the window!" Jess shouts, inching the window down. I pull my arm back. "*Fuck you!*" she shouts, and speeds away as if I am the one who has betrayed her.

A few days later, she is back at the house.

"I'm here for a minute," she says, slamming on the brakes of the car and pulling into the garage. I open the car door and push her away from the ignition, grabbing the car keys and trying to free Bruce, but Jess is quick. She regains her balance, pulls herself up on the steering wheel and pushes me out the door. Tires screeching, she drives away, gravel flying everywhere.

Chapter 4

"I am a nut." In 2015, two years later and after repeated hospitalizations, crisis centers and emergency rooms, Jess is calling from a hospital emergency room in Frankford, Northeast Philadelphia.

"You're not a nut. You're an addict. Using drugs makes you feel nutty and out of control. Everyone feels crazy if they use drugs. You are no exception. Opioids release chemicals that hijack your brain and destroy self-control. Drugs and alcohol are toxic chemicals, and when mixed with heroin laced with fentanyl, a fatal concoction—lethal poisons will kill you. Poisons swirl around in your bloodstream and into your brain, a delicate, three-pound, jelly-like substance, altering the way your brain cells fire and changing the way you think, and pretty quickly, I might add. A cauldron of chemicals firing chaotic, confused messages that make you believe you have to act on the insane message pushing you to use more drugs. In reality, it's the toxic, addicting chemicals that are sending you crazy messages to your brain telling you to *take more drugs, drink more alcohol and you'll feel better.* Faulty messages that say using will stop the cravings. Momentarily, the cravings stop, but they come back more forcefully the next day and the next. Jess, you have to protect your brain! You have to take care of all of your organs, your heart, your lungs, your liver, your entire body! No wonder you feel like a nut."

I'm hoping this umpteenth lecture from me, her mother, someone who loves her unconditionally, will help her to stop taking opioids, benzodiazepines and heroin.

"Xanaz is a benzo too! Don't fool yourself pretending that these drugs are not addictive. They are addictive. All of these toxic substances suppress your breathing. Do you know what happens when your breathing is suppressed?" I ask, not waiting for her answer. "You can die. You are making up reality. You have no idea what you're putting in your mouth." I hear Jess stifle a yawn.

"Are you listening to me?" I ask my daughter. "There are serious side effects, dangers that can be fatal. Ingesting unknown substances can damage every organ and cause liver failure. Expecting your brain, heart and liver to remain healthy while you are taking drugs or drinking alcohol is a fantasy and keeps you in denial about your addiction. Don't fool yourself, Jess! You are an addict. Do you hear me? Do you think about the things I am saying to you? People die every day doing exactly what you are doing, throwing pills down their throats laced with who knows what, shooting drugs into their veins, engaging in high risk, insane behaviors. Taking drugs makes you do things you would not normally do if you were not in the addiction cycle, craving more and more drugs. Like the time you took off your blouse and walked down Broad Street half naked so you could "cool-off." You were high and acting crazy!"

"I was hot, Mom," Jess defends. "It was August. Center City Philadelphia is hot in August."

"Jess, in what universe do people walk down the

street in Center City Philadelphia without a blouse on? When the police officer told you to put your clothes on you were lucky you were not arrested for indecent exposure. What the hell were you thinking of for God's sake? You are begging for trouble Jess, just asking to be arrested. Thank God that girl at the gas station was kind enough to give you money to get home. Crazy behavior Jess, really crazy," I say, exasperated.

"Drugs can put people in a permanent vegetative state. I heard of someone still alive but in a coma for five years from using drugs. *A coma, Jess*, which means he is not going to wake up! He is in a persistent coma. His mother and father cannot take their son off life support and let him die. A nurse takes care of him. The drugs he bought on the street caused brain damage and he is brain dead. Day in, day out he lies there, a thirty-year-old, his heart strong, but he is in a coma. Who knows how long that can go on? He lost consciousness and brain function five years ago. His life is over, but his parents visit every day, hoping he will wake up. The nurse who takes care of him has no idea how long he can live in a vegetative state. He could be in a coma for years. It's already been five years."

"He's been in a coma for five years?" Jess asks, waking up to our conversation.

"Yes, a scary thought. A terrible decision, if not an impossible one for his parents to make—taking their child off life support. His parents pray that that their son will regain consciousness, and grieve the loss of their son every day. Coming out of a persistent coma is possible, but it is very rare. He is young and he could remain unconscious for a long time and eventually die. Think of the pain and grief this family is going through. Addiction leads to death, incarceration, or a mental hospital. Jess, you are batting two out of three.

"Have you ever used a needle to shoot drugs?" I ask, pausing to take a breath.

"No Mom! I would never do that!" My daughter shouts over the phone. "I am afraid of needles. Stop saying awful things." Later, she admits the thought of shooting drugs has crossed her mind. "I don't like to think I'm an addict. I want to think I have control," she says, just as my clients who struggle with drug and alcohol addiction do, especially at the beginning of their recovery when they want to be like everyone else.

"Jess, you want things to be the same way they were before you picked up and used drugs and got addicted, but they can never be the same. Ever! If you don't face what's happening, then you won't get a handle on the fact that you have an addiction. You cannot recover alone. You need help. You are playing a game of Russian roulette. No one wakes up in the morning and says that today is a good day to die! People use heroin and swallow pills laced with poisons because they are addicts. I was married to your father, who was addicted to alcohol and drugs. At the time, I did not understand the way addiction hijacks the brain until I began working at Recovery Inc. I divorced your father because I did not want you to see drugs and alcohol in our home."

At the time, I naively thought that Jess might be spared the same struggle with addiction that her father had, a struggle that destroyed our marriage and our home. I didn't understand the strong genetic component to the disease of addiction.

"I know denial," I say, lecturing my daughter, trying to make her understand. "I was in denial thinking I could stop the influence of your father's addiction by leaving the marriage and getting divorced, out of sight, out of mind, so to speak—denial. "Walking away from you like I did my marriage is not an option," I say, hoping today's lecture will have the power to stop Jess's addiction and cure it. "I will never leave you, but I am not giving you money or allowing you to come home and live in the house while you are using drugs." Always second-guessing myself, questioning whether I am helping my daughter when I buy her cigarettes that she can turn into cash on the streets for drugs. "You need help Jess. I love you, but you need a 12-step program like Alcoholic Anonymous or Narcotic Anonymous. You need a program, meetings or a self-help group. You can't do this alone. It's impossible to do it alone!"

I am a therapist helping others and I can't reach my daughter.

Jess, my only child, is an opioid addict. Before her addiction, Jess was a graduate from the University of California with a degree in business, aspiring to get an MBA or become an entertainment lawyer with a career in film or real estate. Now, all of her goals are replaced by an ongoing daily battle to stop using drugs. Many years into the addiction, she is still using drugs, going from one job to another, her savings spent, car repossessed, broken relationships, family members estranged. She moves from one recovery house to the next, the addiction worse now than it was the day I received the text from her father telling me our daughter was an addict.

"I feel nutty," Jess repeats to me on the cellphone. "I don't know what happened to me. I wanted to stop using, so I threw the drugs away in a trash can on Frankford Avenue in Kensington and stopped all at once. The doctor at the hospital warned me that if you suddenly stop you can become delirious, the reason I ended up in the mental hospital. I didn't know that if you stopped taking everything without a medical detoxification, withdrawal kicks in. A person can become violently ill. That's what happened to me. But now I just want to stop using drugs, Mom. I'm sick of it. I've been to hospital emergency rooms, in-patient hospitals, recovery houses. I have crashed in stranger's apartments not knowing where my next meal is coming from. I've tried living on my own, but I can't do anything without your help. I'm a complete failure, a drug addict, an obsessed person with a one-track mind; my brain tells me to keep the pain of withdrawal away. Remember, Mom, how I had goals and to-do lists. I graduated from college and was applying to graduate schools. I had a desire to be something, to make something of myself. I still want to get married and have a family, but not while I am using drugs. I have to find a way to get better. You have to help me, Mom. You are right, I cannot do this alone."

"You are an addict struggling with the disease of addiction," I tell Jess over and over. "There's a lot to understand about addiction. You need help. We are a society that says, *pull yourself up by your bootstraps, kick yourself in the butt and get better right now*. I used to feel that way, thinking all it took was sheer willpower to get better. If people tried harder and exerted enough strength to stop destructive habits like using drugs or drinking alcohol they could do it. After attending Al-Anon 12-step meetings for family and friends of people struggling with addiction, I learned that it doesn't happen just because we want it to happen. There's a lot to learn about the disease of addiction. In the past, I didn't want to know anything about addiction. I didn't grow up with the disease of addiction and felt above it. In reality I was afraid. Stopping substance abuse is not an act of sheer willpower. It does however include making a decision, outlining a plan of action, guarding one's sobriety by staying away from "people, places and things" from your past. It doesn't happen overnight. Building a relationship with your higher power through daily surrender prayer and meditation is a big part of the process, something to surrender to and lean on, however you may conceptualize a higher power. Reaching out to Alcoholic Anonymous, a fellowship of people that can help you."

I tell this to my daughter knowing that only a strong relationship with other members in a 12-step fellowship of her choosing as well as building a relationship with God can stop the downhill spiral into the hell of addiction. "Get down on your knees and pray," I tell her. "Your addiction brought me to my knees. Even though addiction is a disease process, it is only by the grace of God and total surrender to his will for you can you recover. I took the job working with opioid addicts so I could learn about the disease process. You are my daughter, Jess. I love you more than anyone else in the world, but I can't do the work for you. I can't finish your homework and bring it up to school for you—our pattern in the past. I can't rescue you. I will be there for you, but your recovery is your own hard work."

Chapter 5

"Stop stereotyping her!" I say to Jim, Jess's father.

"She's an addict," Jim says. "She has to hit bottom and be done with the streets and the lifestyle. Only Jess can do it. Everyone's bottom is different. Mine was when you and I separated and divorced. I lost you and Jess, my family. I was living in a studio apartment. I had no friends. You were my best friend from the time I was eighteen years old. I loved your family, especially your father. He was always good to me. He gave me a job at the metal yard where I worked for years. I started to grow up when I worked for him. He trusted me and gave me responsibility. I was connected to your father.

The relationship helped me meet the challenge of the daily grind; going to work and taking care of myself. I sorted and learned how to weld metal, getting it ready for shipments overseas. I was given responsibility. You've known me since I was eighteen years old.

"You remember my father, who was always sitting in that recliner with a glass of scotch with ice," Jim continues. "He was an alcoholic and he died when I was twenty-one years old. I never got to know him. He was always drunk. Your father was different; he went to work every day. He took care of you and your sister even though he and your mom were divorced. He never drank and he once told me, "I only have wine on Passover." Your father meant everything to me. He was the kindest man I have ever known. He was good to everyone, not only to me. You were lucky to have him as a father. My addiction bottom was when I lost my family, you and Jess, and your father too. It was a big loss for me. Raven, I'm grateful that we are still close and remain friends. Jess will have to find her way back from this nightmare and accept that she is an addict. Stop over-protecting Jess. Say it to her straight. Tell her like it is, don't sugar coat it."

"Don't call her an addict, stop labeling her. The

labeling bothers me," I tell Jim, believing I have the power to stop the wreckage from Jess's addiction; a locomotive bearing down on our family, destroying it, tearing it apart. I am Jess's mother. I can magically stop the train wreck by willing it to stop. I raised Jess. I know what's good for her. I can do it. I am her mother! "You would not label a person or withdraw your support from someone who has a disease like diabetes, COPD, or cancer? Before you label her, say she has the disease of addiction. Addiction is a disease and is passed on generationally. *You* have the disease of addiction. By the grace of God and the hard work you did in Alcoholics Anonymous, you now have your disease under control. Our daughter has to get her disease under control."

"Raven, this is the hardest thing I have ever been through, seeing our daughter struggle with addiction like I did," Jim replies. "She is my child too, but I have to say it like it is. If I don't, then I am in denial about the difficulty of addiction and the long process of recovery. Saying it straight makes it real for me. Neither you nor I nor anyone has control over Jess. It is sad and frightening. I am scared for her. Every day I wake up and I pray for her, what else can I do? Give her money? No, I won't do that. I buy her cigarettes. I know she can trade them on the street but that's as far as I go. So say it like it is, Raven. Jess is an addict. Our daughter is an addict! Yes, she has the disease of addiction, as you so formally put it. Of course she has the disease of addiction. Your work as a therapist requires that you present a professional framework for your clients to understand their disease of addiction, but I was out there on the streets. I know what it takes to stop drinking and using drugs. I *know* what it takes to hit bottom and crawl out of that hole. There's a point of acceptance that a person has to get to about their addiction, and Jess is not there yet. She is not there! She has not hit her bottom."

"What point is that?" I ask, exhausted from the conversation. I want Jess's father to stop calling Jess an addict without reminding our daughter that it is a disease process! I want him and everyone to acknowledge that it is a disease like cancer, Alzheimer's, or COPD, not a moral failing.

Her father continues, "It's an acceptance that her addiction is a serious problem that she has to deal with through life. Jess can never pick up a drink or use drugs. Acceptance is a hard point for an addict to get to. Raven, say it straight so you don't stay stuck in denial. Denial is a problem too. Our child is sick. Say it like it is Raven, so she hears you. Her mind has been hijacked by drugs. Her rational mind is gone. Her goals of being a real estate developer, a film writer, or having a business right now are gone. She tells herself that she can control her addiction with minimal outside help. She tells herself that she can stop using and do it on her own. Her self-talk is made up of, "I have will power. I can do it on my own." She is willful and arrogant, all part of the disease process of addiction. If by some miracle she is able to get her addiction under control without doing the 12-step work going to meetings, working the 12 steps, getting a sponsor to help guide her, she might be able to stop using, but she would be a "dry drunk." Her personality would be the same, self-centered and headstrong. For most people struggling with addiction it's not easy to stop using drugs or drinking alcohol. There may be that one person who can stop cold turkey and never pick up again, but that is a rare person. There's a lot of work for a person to do on their personality after they stop drinking or drugging. They may not pick up, but dry drunks are not nice to be around with their smug attitudes and behaviors similar to when they were using drugs. This is not a bag of potato chips or chocolate chip cookies that Jess craves and must put down and walk away from."

My ex is driving *his* point home, but I am still determined to stop the labeling of my daughter and set the record straight. Jess has the disease of addiction just like her father had. My ex-husband Jim, Jess's father, was once addicted to heroin and alcohol, a disease he was able to get a handle on over forty years ago and recover from with help from the Alcoholics Anonymous 12-step program. At the time, we were married. He was living at home with a roof over his head and food on the table. Jess is living in recovery houses in Kensington, known as the "badlands" for drugs and addiction in Philadelphia and in the United States. When I was married to Jess's father, I distanced myself from the overwhelming process and eventually divorced him. I wanted the addiction to disappear. Forty years later, many years after the divorce, I still do not know the details of my ex-husband's recovery and the Alcoholics Anonymous program that he embraced. When Jess was a child, my mission—my role as Jess's mother—was to protect our daughter from seeing alcohol or drugs in our home, and yet Jess is now living in Kensington, moving from one recovery house to the next. My precious only child, my daughter Jess, is living in a heavily infested drug area and I am helpless to do anything about it. Dreams of success for my daughter are gone, replaced by wanting her to simply stay alive and live a sober life.

"Our daughter is not an addict. She is struggling with the disease of addiction," I quietly repeat to Jim, insisting on political correctness, ashamed of the stereotyping and the labeling of our daughter being an addict. At the beginning of her addiction, I was absolutely certain our daughter would easily recover. She was smart and wise. She would do what she needed to recover and move on. Now, after the "delirium," as the psychiatrist at Kirkbride, a mental hospital and drug treatment facility called it, a "drug-induced psychosis," a break from reality. Her opioid addiction is out of control and Jess is unrecognizable. "Powerful, cunning, and baffling," the Alcoholics Anonymous Big Book for recovery says. Jess is an unrecognizable person standing on street corners smoking cigarettes, hat turned backwards looking cool, yet pleading to me, her mother, on the phone saying, "I can't take it anymore. I don't know what to do. I need to come home. I want to come home. I have lost my willpower. I need help. Can you help me Mom? I cannot stay in hospitals or recovery houses anymore."

Chapter 6

"Why don't we pay for a thirty-day treatment stay?" I ask Jim. "You will be wasting your thirty thousand dollars," Jess's father says, worried our daughter's insurance won't cover the long recovery road ahead.

Jess has finally explored her insurance recovery options. "My insurance will cover a sober living house in Bucks County," she says. Realizing she cannot come home, Jess is being released from the hospital to a recovery house. With the help of a social worker, she is searching for places that take her new insurance.

"After thirty days, when the black-out period at the recovery house is over, I can have my car, get a job and drive myself to work. Can I have the car Mom? I was making payments on the Subaru too," Jess says calling from the hospital. "The social worker will get me into a recovery house in Bucks County. There are a lot of recovery houses in Bucks County. Once the thirty-day black-out period is over I can get a job and drive to work. Besides, I'll be out of the recovery house in no time! I know I can beat this. I can stop the addiction. The social worker at the hospital today told me that it costs five-hundred dollars a month to live at the Bensalem Recovery House I'm looking into, an out-of-pocket expense. Will you help me pay for the recovery house?"

Jess is beginning her recovery journey with new hope, and so are we. She is calling from the Bensalem Recovery House.

"I was offered a job today near the Bensalem Recovery House. I am the only person here who graduated from college and the only one who doesn't have a felony on her record. It's going to be easy to get a job, Mom. I can do this. I am going to 12-step meetings. I already have a sponsor. My sponsor thinks I should take this job. It's an assistant manager position. I am going to take it. I can do this. I can beat this addiction."

"After the black-out period ends you can have your car," I tell her. "The condition is to stay sober and pay part of your rent. We will help you, but you have to take responsibility too."

Jess is certain she will get a handle on her addiction quickly and so are we. When our daughter was in college in California she lived a sober life. She paid her bills and her life was in order. Now she is struggling with addiction and I want to be done with it, tired of living with the uncertainty, wishing life could go back to normal, but there is nothing I can do to make her recovery move faster. I am learning that life will never be the same.

A few days later Jess phones...

"This place sucks. The people in the recovery house make fun of me. No one is like me. I'm the only college graduate. I haven't been to jail. I can't relate to anyone. I want to move out of the recovery house or come home right now. Another possibility is I could move into a private room with a woman from the Alcoholics Anonymous program, someone I met at an AA meeting. She rents out rooms in her home for the price we pay the recovery house. The one rule is no drugs or alcohol, and I won't use drugs. I promise. I will never use drugs again. I'm serious this time Mom."

"Stay a bit longer where you are and try," we suggest, but Jess is adamant. "I'm leaving," she says. "The girls here make fun of me. I hate them. They tell me I have a long road to go and that I will relapse again. That isn't encouraging. Besides, what do they know? They have relapsed many times. I won't relapse again, I know it! I want out! If you don't pick me up I'm packing my things and walking to this woman's place from AA and taking the private room. I'll figure it out. I'm taking the assistant manager position so I will have money to be on my own. I won't need your help."

"Geez Jess, Can't you give it one more day?" Her father and I ask.

"No," Jess is adamant. "I'm walking down the road now to the main highway. I don't care if I sleep in the woods."

"Okay, we will be there to help you move. Go back and pack up your things."

"Thanks Mom. I have to do laundry first. I'll have everything packed. We can stop at the Laundromat then I'll go to the new place."

Jess is waiting outside the recovery house with a black plastic trash bag filled with dirty laundry and her suitcase. "This is the last time we pick you up and move you," we tell our daughter. "Phone ahead and tell this woman you will be there. We will give you a check and you can pay us back when you start work."

A few weeks later, she phones. "Come pick me up. I relapsed again. I am depressed. The woman I was renting a room from, the one in Alcoholics Anonymous asked me to leave. I broke her rule by smoking pot. I'm not using now so I don't understand why she can't let me stay and give me a second chance. Besides smoking pot is nothing. It's legal in some states, but she doesn't care. I don't know why she is making such a big deal. I'm lonely, Mom. Can I come home?"

So begins our long journey from one recovery house, friend's apartments, emergency rooms, psychiatric hospitals to the next, but Jess cannot come home. We drop off groceries at the places where she lives. We pay her rent, only to be greeted with yet another call, "Come and get me, I relapsed. I need help." "We will come pick you up shortly," I leave a message on Jess's phone. "Your father and stepmother have stopped by to talk and console."

"What did I do wrong?" I ask Jim and Harriet, Jess's stepmother. "I took good care of Jess, fed her tofu hotdogs, made sure she stayed in touch with both of you, hoping for a good father-daughter relationship. She never saw any drinking in the home. I tried my best, but apparently it was not good enough," I tell them. They are both longtime members of the Alcoholic Anonymous 12-step program.

While I was raising Jess, my kitchen cabinets overflowed with vitamins placed in neat rows on the white Formica counter behind the Green Star juicer used to make organic wheat grass juice mixed with organic kale, celery, carrots, blueberries, cucumbers and a host of other organic protein foods. My daughter grew up eating organic food, instilling a healthy respect for the body as the temple to the soul. Her face crunched, holding her nose, she drank the healthy green concoction. For lunch the meal was Morning Star veggie burgers, organic vegetables with a side of couscous for dinner.

When Jess came home from school she played outside. At dusk, after the children in the neighborhood went home to do their homework, she sat at the dining room table or in front of the TV and did her homework. When my daughter began elementary school, her finished homework was placed in the book bag at the front door for her to take to school. There was a consistent routine at bedtime, teeth brushed and a nighttime story. She grew up in a holistic home with an emphasis on natural cures. There were no drugs or alcohol in our home. She went with me to yoga classes and crystal healing workshops. She learned about the power of positive self-talk, affirmations and visualization. She accompanied me to spiritual groups held in community centers, churches and hotel banquet rooms. During the healing workshops she played with her Lego set while I facilitated groups on how to heal the body, mind and spirit.

When my daughter was three years old, I searched for answers to my failing marriage. Jess and I traveled to the Philippines to see the psychic surgeons, healers who claimed to heal the body by the laying-on of hands. My daughter was always by my side. During the summer, at a Poconos Mountain retreat, she participated in weekends of meditation and prayer and ate macrobiotic food. We flew to Hawaii for meditation workshops. At thirteen years old she was introduced to a group that studied past lives and dreams. Together we continued the childhood tradition of exploring our psychological selves at night through dreams and sharing them in the morning. Determined to protect her from the nightmare of her father's addiction, I pretended everything was all right in the marriage yet secretly threw away empty liquor bottles and bags of white powder along with cone-shaped newspapers and needles hidden behind the toilet on the windowsill. My daughter would not be exposed to her father's addiction.

When Jess was older and I could no longer hide her father's addiction from her or cope with it, I divorced her dad, certain I was making the right decision. It was better to be a single parent and raise Jess alone. She would live with me and identify with my values. I didn't use drugs or smoke pot. If Jess loved me the way I loved my father, she would not want to disappoint me. She would naturally stay away from dangerous situations including drugs and alcohol. She would trust the love she and I shared and withstand peer pressure, always making good decisions or conferring with me if she felt conflicted.

"Wasn't I a good role model, never drinking alcohol, only using holistic modalities for healing, not prescription drugs or street drugs of any kind sending

Jess to the best private schools?" I ask her father and stepmother.

"The same school she couldn't wait to leave and dropped out of in eleventh grade declaring she would never go back," they both remind me.

"You didn't do anything wrong, Raven," Jess's stepmother Harriet says to soothe me. "Jess has had addictive personality traits since she was born."

Chapter 7

Four years since the addiction came to light, the cellphone is ringing with an urgency I am wearily familiar with.

"Jess is calling again," I tell Bruce, my daughter's dog that now lives with me. He blinks; soft, moist brown eyes flutter open and close quickly. Sighing, he goes back to sleep.

"Not answering the cell!" I tell Bruce, rubbing my foot on his belly, thumbing through the pages of the latest issue of *Psychology Today*. Bruce, a mixed breed of Chow (protective) Keeshond (sweet) and Shepherd (guard dog) is one in a line of my daughter's many pets left behind for me to raise. Rolling the pillow up and around my ears, I drown out the sound of the cellphone's incessant ringing demanding I pick up and answer it right now! Exhausted, I sink into the bed and think about the few times I have said "no" to my daughter.

"No," I do not want another bunny, cat, or hamster.

"No," I will not take care of another stray animal you found or decided on a whim to buy from Monster Pet (Bruce).

"No, I do not want a twelve-week-old puppy," I said the day I visited Jess's South Philadelphia apartment, one of many places she lived while struggling with her addiction. Bending down, petting silky puppy fur, breathing in sweet puppy breath, I pick up the adorable puppy, put him in his makeshift crate, and walk to the front door.

"Hey, come back!" Jess races to the front door and blocks the exit, arms folded across her chest. "You can't leave without Bruce. I thought you'd be happy to have company. Besides, I have to go to work!"

"You should have thought of your work schedule before you paid five-hundred dollars to Monster Pet for a dog you can't take care of and decided I would want! I work every day too! What kind of a breed is an Eshland anyway?" I ask, eyeing the pedigree papers on the front table next to the door stating Bruce is a pedigree Eshland, a breed known for its gentle nature, a mixture of Border Collie and Terrier (a breed I never heard of and can't find on the web).

"His name is Bruce," Jess says, letting me know the dog is here to stay. "He's seven weeks old. At six months old, I will put him in a doggie daycare or get a pet sitter. Don't worry, it's not forever." I calculate another out-of-pocket expense.

"You are cute," I whisper to Bruce, who is running around in circles banging against the sides of the crate, clawing to get out. He paws the front of the crate and it springs open. Free at last, the puppy dashes towards me and nips at my feet.

"Hi little guy," I say, picking him up. A few months later Bruce moves in with me, animal number seven that Jess can no longer take care of—so much for saying no. The brown and black puppy looks up at me through a thick mane of soft fur. Nature drew two perfect bulls' eyes around Bruce's dark brown eyes. Bruce is more shy and sweet than protective. In the morning, he inches across the body pillow that divides the queen size bed in half. With Bruce it is love at first sight.

"This is your side of the bed," I tell Bruce at night, pointing to the other side of the ten-foot-long body pillow, a body divider bought at Cuddledown. "Your side," I say, pointing to his side of the bed. "This is my side, this is your side." The puppy nudges my hand and paws at the down pillow, slowly inching over to my side of the bed. I pat the pillow, encouraging him to visit me. Bruce climbs up and over the body pillow and licks my face. I pull him close to me.

On our nighttime walks, his tail wagging, his tongue, with the black mark in the center marking him as a protective Chow breed, hangs out of the corner of his mouth. He sniffs the ground until he catches the scent of a fox or the familiar smell of a neighborhood dog and lunges, dragging me up the street.

"You're not a good boy!" I say, shaking my finger, gripping the leash, trying to keep my balance. Bruce is satisfied. He chased the intruder away and turns his attention towards home.

Once again, the incessant ringing of the cellphone interrupts my daydreaming. It stops and starts again. Am I on speed dial? I'm certain that it is Jess calling the way I know when I'm getting sick—a sinking feeling in my belly, my hands and face wet and clammy, chills rise and fall. My head aches. My stomach is in knots. I wipe my clammy hands on my nightshirt and slide my feet into brown clogs. The ringing is begging me to answer it, but not today. Today is Sunday. My day off!

A bright Sunday morning, sunlight streams into the bedroom. I am making a to-do list organizing my day. If I pick-up the phone Jess will say, "Everything is good Mom, all good, no problems," hollow words. "How's Bruce? How are you, Mom? I miss you. How's the B dog? I worry about him, worry about you too Mom. Is he all right Mom? Are you okay? Can you hold the leash when you walk Bruce? Wrap it around your hand and don't let him get away from you. I worry about you, especially in the winter with slippery black ice and snow. Are you okay?"

The shrill sound of the cellphone is pleading with me to answer it, but it is Sunday. *My time*, I think focusing on my Al-Anon recovery, my 12-step program, the sister program to Alcoholics Anonymous. Al-Anon is for loved ones, friends and relatives of family members struggling with addiction.

"Put the oxygen mask on yourself first," I am

reminded at every Al-Anon meeting I attend four times a week; a place to talk about the pain and struggle of watching a loved one struggle with addiction. *You can't do anything about the person wrestling with addiction, but you can change yourself, your attitude, your addiction to your loved one's recovery and need to change their behaviors. Contain the automatic response, the knee-jerk reaction. Become aware of the way you respond to situations.*

In the meeting, hands folded, eyes averted, I silently shout, "But *I am her mother. You could not possibly understand unless you are a parent of a child who has an addiction. Do you have any idea what it is like to be the mother of an addicted child who was raised in suburbia and is now living on the streets of Kensington in North Philadelphia; different than a spouse who comes home drunk and sleeps on the couch, but I know about that too. At least her father had a roof over his head and a bed to sleep on when he passed out on the couch. I hope you never know what it's like to be a single mother raising a child alone and hear the words your daughter is addicted to opioids!*

When I could no longer tolerate or hide her father's addiction throwing out empty alcohol bottles, cocaine and dirty heroin needles hidden behind the toilet, drug paraphernalia left on the ledge in a moldy corner in the bathroom, empty bottles tossed on the floor in the first-floor apartment in center city Philadelphia. Jess's father shooting heroin behind the thick bar glass single bathroom window, away from the prying eyes of passers-by, unaware, like I was, of his addiction. In 1967, at twenty-years old, when I met Jess's father, I did not know that addiction was a disease, something I had no control of and that ran in his family. What I did know was that a few years after my marriage to Jim in 1976 when I was twenty-nine years old, I wanted out of the marriage. At thirty-three years old, after Jess was born, I wanted a divorce from Jim. The disease of alcoholism and addiction had nothing to do with me or the way I had grown up. It had taken its toll on our family. Years went by before I could say goodbye to my daughter's father, a man who was my best friend and husband. A man I met when he was eighteen years old. Someone I married whose family I lived with on summer breaks from college because his family was more familiar to me than my own, except for the drinking, which was foreign to me. I grew up in an alcohol-free home. After Jess was born, not wanting her exposed to alcohol and drugs and tired of hiding the problem from my family, I left the marriage. I was finished and finally able to go on with my life away from the disease of addiction.

Chapter 8

The cellphone continues to ring. My body aches. A fever is on the way, a scratchy throat, my temples throb. I pull the covers over my head, tears rolling out of the corners of my eyes. There is no time to get sick. I have to work, pay bills, take care of the house. Draping my arm over my forehead, I wipe the tears away and listen to the relentless ringing of the cell. Jess is now thirty-seven years old and she's been living in recovery houses for several years. She is not allowed to come home.

A voice shouts "Get up and pay attention to me now! Pick me up! Take care of me! Don't you love me! You are the only person I have in the world who can help me. You are the only person who understands me and takes care of me! I don't know what to do, Mom, help me! I can't live in Kensington in filthy recovery houses infested with bed bugs and people who throw water in my bed at night while I sleep. I am scared Mom. Come get me. Come now! I cannot stay here. I cannot live here."

A wave of guilt, nausea and sickness washes over me.

What if my daughter is in the hospital? People die every day in Philadelphia from a drug overdose.

In 2017 there were 1,217 opioid deaths; 2018 had 1,116, and in 2019 1,150 in Philadelphia (estimates). In 2019 overdose deaths were mostly in the 35-44 age range, my daughter's age range—death caused by drugs, heroin, fentanyl and benzodiazepines, her drugs of choice.[1]

Get up and answer the damn phone. We are in the middle of a heroin epidemic and you are in bed reading *Psychology Today*, waiting for the phone to stop ringing! Remember Ryan, the red haired, freckle-faced girl from grade school? Where is Ryan now?

"You'll be dead and looking up from inside a wooden box like your friend Ryan," Jess's father says,

---

1. https://www.addictioncenter.com/news/2020/03/philly-opioid-strategies-kensington/

hoping the scare tactic will make Jess stop using drugs. His strong parental voice falls on deaf ears.

"It's a game of Russian roulette." Her father's voice is straining, hoping parental words of wisdom have a magical power that can stop the downhill spiral and stop Jess's life from spinning out of control. His words are filled with fear and longing that his daughter will stop using heroin, opiates, Benzos the same way he was able to stop forty years ago. *"You are powerless,"* I think, but say nothing to Jess's father, knowing Al-Anon wisdom will fall on deaf ears. Al-Anon philosophy will not be heard. Her father's Alcoholic Anonymous wisdom is failing with our daughter as well.

"You can get a handle on this addiction. Go to AA meetings, get a sponsor and work the program like I did! Well actually," Jess's father adds shyly, "I worked the First Step, *I am powerless over alcohol and my life had become unmanageable.* If I pick up a drink or do drugs I will be back where I was forty years ago, digging myself out of a hole. You were only two years old, too young to recall the friends from Alcoholics Anonymous that came to the house and later became my friends, the men who took me to St. Mary's detox center and later to Fairmount Hospital and AA meetings." His voice is rising with fear, remembering the days he bought drugs on Brown Street and Wallace Street in Philadelphia, the men in AA who saved his life and later helped him get into Fairmount hospital where he was admitted, an AA fellowship of friends. The Alcoholics Anonymous fellowship of support—Jess's father's lifeline. As I watched from the sidelines my only goal was to protect my daughter, end the marriage and get a divorce. There was nothing I could do for my husband, in the same way there is nothing I can do for Jess. In Al-Anon I have learned to keep the focus on myself, take care of myself, let go and pray and strengthen my faith turning my will over to the care of God that guides and protects. *Does God hear my prayers? I think sitting in Al-Anon meetings. Please protect my daughter. I know you watch over the world and I am one small person. Please hear my prayers. Please take care of Jess.*

Chapter 9

"Yes, I can work in a drug and alcohol group practice," I say in a job interview I am applying for as a mental health drug and alcohol counselor. "I know about addiction and mental health," I tell the interviewer, thinking about Jess's disease of addiction and undiagnosed depression as well as her father's drug and alcohol use and depression too. In 2015, I am sixty-eight years old, and I am hired to work with homeless men and women struggling with substance abuse, many of whom were recently released to the outpatient drug and alcohol group practice, my new job. After being hired, writing my notes on each client after the session, identifying "triggers" to relapse, I review the treatment plan and goals with the client to help prevent relapse and strengthen their recovery, helping them make a connection from past addictive destructive behaviors to healthier behaviors and identifying the stressors in their life, triggers for relapse, and obstacles to recovery. As a drug and alcohol counselor, I teach clients to be proactive and manage stress, emphasizing self-care.

"Be proactive. Ask yourself what might happen when you go to a Sunday family dinner or barbeque and wine is served. How will you manage the family outing when you're looking at the cooler filled with cold beer?"

"An ice-cold beer is a trigger for me," clients say. "Beer commercials are a trigger for me. The heat of the summer is a trigger. I go to the All Family Bar with discounted ribs and a beer on Tuesdays and Thursdays, sit in the dark, fade into the background and cool off with a beer." All are triggers for my clients—a hot summer day, family events, beer commercials, the heat, are all triggers to relapse. In my private and group practice, I help clients identify negative thinking styles that lead to relapse, explaining Symptoms of Post-Acute Withdrawal (PAWS) that happen after a person has stopped drinking or using drugs and is recovering. The mental fogginess that clients experience and their inability to concentrate is a normal initial response. The brain is beginning its healing process. Without the use of drugs or alcohol to manage stress and calm cravings, when people stop using, symptoms of PAWS can occur. Clients are beginning a new, fragile first stage of recovery. Feelings no longer masked by using can be overwhelming. Difficulty concentrating is common. Controlling repetitive negative thinking is a challenge. All of these can lead to relapse.

I tell my clients: "You have to manage your stress. Go for a brisk walk. Oxygenate the blood and release endorphins into the body, nature's natural analgesic. The brain will be stimulated in a new way. When you go for a walk or begin a routine of daily meditation, endorphins are released, the feel-good chemical that supports the healing process and fires healthier messages to your brain. As you create new positive habits, be consistent and set a schedule that works for you. Drink water, not sodas. Limit caffeine, go for a swim or to a Pilates class, or practice yoga. Sit still and meditate. Do things in moderation but emphasize consistency. Don't pick up and use substances no matter how you feel or what is going on. You will get triggered in life," I tell my clients. "Life is hard. People and events can make us feel emotionally reactive. We want to respond or use drugs or drink alcohol to take away unpleasant feelings. Doing new positive activities creates new healthier neural pathways in the brain and positive mental responses. The brain is changing, and you, by your efforts, are creating new positive habits."

"What do you do to manage your stress?" clients ask.

"I go for a walk, meditate, rest, watch TV, pick up the phone and call someone I trust who won't shame or blame me when I share my feelings with them. I don't buy into every negative thought and demand my mind makes. I passively observe negative self-talk, thoughts that can take me down a dark, self-destructive road. I go through a consistent meditation practice at least once a day for twenty to thirty minutes, I train my brain to become an observer of my thoughts, to let thoughts come and go, to passively observe them. My suggestion is that when you feel emotionally reactive, do something different. If you do the same behaviors you will get the same results. When you feel upset go for a walk, pick up the phone, call a friend—do anything positive, but don't drink or use drugs. Obsessive negative thoughts are demanding and can encourage you to pick up and use. I tell myself that negative compelling thoughts will pass, and they do. Sometimes you have to push hard through them. But you are never alone. There is always someone to reach out to—recovery folks, clergy, friend, or family. As you continue in your recovery you may have dreams of smoking a joint, drinking, or using drugs. This is normal. There is scientific proof that meditating and breathing deeply, closing one's eyes for ten to twenty minutes each day, saying a soothing, healing word like "relax" or following one's breath, inhaling and exhaling, integrates the right and left sides of the brain. Eventually thoughts and nighttime dreams of using can fade."

City Behavioral Health (CBH) in Philadelphia, the insurance company that pays for Medicaid clients, wants therapists to teach mindfulness meditation, an evidence-based meditation and stress reduction technique to help reduce stress. "Take a breath in and exhale through your mouth twice as long, and repeat this process. When you meditate, keep it simple. Say a word like joy, relax, peace, surrender. Observe your thoughts flow in and out of your mind. Notice the way you feel and the sounds around you. Let the sounds drift in and out of your mind." This is what I explain when teaching mindfulness meditation and other simple meditation techniques, hoping that something will be interesting for a client and take hold helping them manage their stress and change the negative patterns in the brain that lead towards relapse.

"One of the most important things to remember" I tell clients, "is to contain the immediate response to pick up and use drugs. Come out of denial as quickly as possible. You can never have just one drink and maintain sobriety. Contain the impulse to pick up a beer or smoke marijuana or take opioids. Slow down the adrenaline reaction from a triggering thought or an emotional response from someone you don't like. Control your thoughts that tell you getting high will feel good and that you can stop using after one time. If someone hurts your feelings or you feel angry, instead of blaming yourself or someone else, go for a walk and do deep breathing. Use self-talk and say, "I don't have to pick up a drink or smoke marijuana, just for today." Take it one moment at a time as suggested in mindfulness practices and 12-step programs. One day at a time. Most importantly, share your feelings.

Reach out to others. When we don't share our feelings, our daily struggles, hurt and pain pile up inside of us. Then we may begin to withdraw or isolate. Emotions are bottled up and we get jammed up inside. This can be a trigger for relapse. Recovery is fragile and leaves one vulnerable to relapse and to another "run," but perhaps not another recovery."

I might have another run for drugs inside me, but not another recovery, clients say.

"It is a lifetime struggle that with patience, persistence, and abstinence gets better over time. One you have to be vigilant about, but it does get easier. There is a point where you can put it behind you but you can never forget," Jim says. You can never use drugs or drink alcohol, even just one time socially, or smoke a joint no matter how tempting it might be. In recovery, you are always practicing Step 1, *I am powerless over alcohol, and my life has become unmanageable.* "We can't throw our arms up in the air and high-five each other and believe we have graduated, deluding ourselves into believing that we can go on that vacation and have a glass of wine or two on the cruise or at the barbeque. This is denial and unrealistic thinking. When a person accepts the reality that they can never use drugs of any kind anywhere, a new way of life can begin, with miracles.

"Marijuana may now be legal in many states, implying the risks are minimal, but this is not true, especially for someone with addiction," I tell my clients. THC, the main active ingredient, changes the brain. "Cognitive impairments in adult rats exposed to THC during adolescence are associated with structural and functional changes in the hippocampus. Studies in adolescent rats exposed to THC are associated with an altered reward system, increasing the likelihood that an animal will self-administer other drugs (e.g., heroin) when given an opportunity."[2]

Drugs and alcohol change the brain and can increase mental illness. In the process, destructive behaviors related to substance abuse result. An individual gets caught in the cycle of addiction that leads to problems with the legal system, creating the inevitable downhill spiral. Like a tornado that destroys everything in its path, addiction uproots and destroys the person, their family and relationships. The person using substances can end up in jail or dead.

---

2. https://www.drugabuse.gov/publications/research-reports/marijuana/what-are-marijuanas-long-term-effects-brain

"For the addict or alcoholic, it is hard to come to terms with never having one glass of wine or beer or smoking marijuana recreationally. Observing clients in therapy and those attending 12-step meetings and people receiving treatment through Medical Assisted Treatments (MAT) like methadone, the difficulty of accepting the fact that they can never pickup a drink or use drugs is one of the reasons people relapse. People test the waters to see if they can control the addiction by drinking just one glass of wine or smoking marijuana," I tell my clients, and Jess.

"I'll relax with a drink or smoke a joint just this one time," clients say. People struggling with addiction delude themselves into thinking that they have the willpower to stop. This is an illusion. The outcome is relapse. Down the rabbit hole a person goes, often leading to death. As the person continues the cycle of recovery to relapse back to recovery and then relapse again, the brain cells associated with addiction get stronger. Life on the street becomes a bleak existence; buying and selling drugs becomes the norm. The dealer makes money and moves on to the next desperate person, but for the person who picks up and uses and goes into respiratory distress, especially if the drug is laced, as heroin often is, with Fentanyl, and if immediate help doesn't come in the form of someone administering CPR or a drug that treats narcotic overdose like Narcan, that person will die.

Family members who struggle to understand addiction say, "I can have one beer or one glass of wine, smoke a joint and get high and not use any drugs for months." My response to family members is that this may be true for someone who doesn't have a predisposition towards addiction. For a person with addiction problems, it is hard, if not impossible, to walk away. Addiction is a brain disease—physical, emotional and spiritual. Any pleasurable activity, including using drugs, stimulates the reward center in the brain. Dopamine is released, another feel-good chemical, and the action wants to be repeated. Opioids increase the amount of dopamine released from the reward center and the demand for dopamine in the brain keeps rising. The reward center in the brain, the pleasure center that tells us when something feels good, secretes ten times more dopamine when using drugs than it would with another feel-good activity like exercise or meditation. In a quest to drink like everyone else or party recreationally with drugs, the person with addiction responds to the flooding of dopamine's increased cravings by using more drugs. Snorting heroin just doesn't do it. Shooting drugs is the next step to get the high.

Addictive drugs can release two to ten times the amount of dopamine that natural rewards do, and they do it fast. Dopamine, one of the "happy chemicals" along with endorphins, serotonin, and oxytocin, is released into the blood stream and activates the reward center in the brain. A person feels euphoric. Fentanyl, a synthetic opioid, is one hundred times stronger than morphine, and is often mixed with street heroin to "cut it" so more profit is made from each sale of this deadly drug, increasing the high. Fentanyl is stronger than heroin. These two potent drugs, fentanyl and heroin, combined with other lethal chemicals to increase profits, can include battery acid or whatever else a drug dealer wants to add to the heroin for distribution, are sold to the unwary buyer. Another danger is stopping using all at once or picking up after a period of abstinence. The opioid receptor sites in the brain have quieted down and are dormant. When a person picks up and uses, the opioid receptor sites, like soldiers who have been waiting to be called back into action, lineup and immediately respond with a bigger demand for more opiates. The body is not used to substances in any amount, so this often leads to overdose and death.

In the 1960s, drugs were part of the counter-culture youth movement. Experimenting with drugs was prevalent. I smoked pot and tried amphetamines but quickly discovered that pot increased my paranoia. I endured an unpleasant high and had to wait for it to end, but I needed something to give me energy and keep me engaged during the day while attending boring college classes. Amphetamines were appealing. Fortunately, I never got hooked on any speedy substance, although I enjoyed the lift.

But soon, I noticed an increased dependency. It was subtle, but scary. I left college and went home to see a former therapist. After that visit I let go of drug use. "People with the disease of addiction cannot walk away," I tell families torn apart by addiction, worn out, frustrated and scared, struggling to understand their loved one's addiction. "When a person uses opioids, receptor sites in the brain multiply and grow like weeds. Like any disease left untreated, it gets worse and could lead to death. The brain is hijacked by drugs, and addiction takes hold."

"Isn't it a choice to pickup and use drugs and drink alcohol?" family members ask. "They are making a choice to use drugs."

People struggling with addiction crave more. "I can do small amounts of heroin and benzodiazepines. I have control and can stop whenever I want to stop," clients say. "Denial is a defense mechanism that all of us resort to when we don't want to face reality," I tell them. "While the brain is remarkably complex, the neurochemical drivers of happiness are quite easy to identify. Dopamine, serotonin, and oxytocin make up the *Happiness Trifecta*. Any activity that increases the production of these neurochemicals will cause a boost in mood."[3]

All three neurochemicals are released when a person uses drugs. The idea that you can use drugs and stay in control of your mind and body is an illusion. People lose control quickly—one of the reasons that for the past several decades there has been an opioid crisis around the world, and especially in the United States. Philadelphia has more opioid-related deaths than any other city in the United States. A person who uses

---

3. https://www.psychologytoday.com/us/blog/vitality/201404/the-neuroscience-giving#:~:text=While%20the%20brain%20is%20remarkably,cause%20a%20boost%20in%20mood.&text=Dopamine%20is%20connected%20to%20motivation%20and%20arousa.

drugs loses the ability to choose. Addiction happens fast—if it feels this good, then more is better. People ignore the changes in their mind and body. Human beings like a natural high, one of the reasons people take up running or swimming. Endorphins, natural analgesics, are released in the brain when we exercise or do other activities, giving us positive feedback so the action will be repeated. Positive action drives the brain towards positive plasticity and builds good habits. Using drugs or doing other negative behaviors like smoking, for example, drives the brain towards negative habits, negative plasticity. The brain is equally good at reinforcing both positive and negative habits.

When a person uses drugs, opioid receptor sites crave more feel-good chemicals and the results are increased use of opioids to keep the cravings in check. Addiction has taken hold, and smaller doses of pills and snorting heroin don't do it. They don't get high anymore. They seek different, stronger combinations of drugs, mixing and matching, making lethal cocktails that could kill them. The opioid receptor sites, like greedy, hungry monsters, proliferate and grow rapidly and duplicate themselves, taking away a person's will. Cravings become stronger and more demanding to the point where a person uses drugs to keep the symptoms of withdrawal at bay. The desire to avoid withdrawal and the flu-like symptoms that accompany it predominates. An addicted person picks up a drug and uses to keep from getting sick.

"I don't want to be sick," clients say when they relapse. "I miss the excitement of the lifestyle," is another lament. To support their habit, drug seeking continues endangering people. To support their addiction, people resort to stealing and lying behaviors not exhibited when they are sober, and relapse deepens. People are ashamed of their inability to control their disease and their behaviors. They are ashamed of the constant relapsing and the guilt that comes with every relapse.

"Drug use and drinking alcohol can begin when a person is young and the brain is still developing. Smoking marijuana during adolescence changes one's brain, making it easier for stronger drugs like heroin to act quickly and cause addiction. The receptor sites are willing and able to respond. In adolescence, when a person uses, they spring into action," I tell clients.

"Why can't I just stop?" People caught in the cycle of addiction ask. Addiction exerts a powerful influence on the brain that manifests in three distinct ways: "craving for the object of addiction, loss of control over its use, and continuing involvement with it." [4] While overcoming addiction is possible, the process is often long, slow, and complicated despite adverse consequences.

"I want to stop using," my daughter said, and so do my clients. "This is the tenth or twentieth time I have relapsed." A person may want to stop using drugs or drinking alcohol, but they can't without help. A person needs a medically assisted detoxification to stop using drugs or drinking alcohol. They should never try to do it on their own.

A person's will to make rational decisions is weakened. Stopping cold turkey is dangerous and can cause horrific flu-like symptoms—nausea, vomiting, muscle cramps, joint pains "times a million," clients report in therapy sessions. People caught in addiction tell themselves that they will stop using tomorrow. Irrational thinking deludes a person into believing they are in control. Instead, they sink deeper and deeper into the addiction. Clients believe they can control the process of drinking or doing drugs. They tell

---

4. https://www.helpguide.org/harvard/how-addiction-hijacks-the-brain.htm

themselves they can use just one more time. Recovery will start tomorrow. Addiction overpowers a person's mind, body and soul; it's difficult for people with the disease of addiction to let go of the illusion that they have control over their disease and can drink or party recreationally. According to the latest government statistics, "in 2018, 67,367 drug overdoses occurred in the United States."[5] With so many deaths, families and loved ones are the collateral damage, the people standing helplessly on the sidelines struggling with the loss of their loved one through addiction.

"I can be like everyone else," people with addiction problems tell themselves. "I'm not like other people in Alcoholics Anonymous or Narcotics Anonymous. I can drink one drink, smoke just one joint and nothing bad is going to happen to me. I'm normal." Wanting to be normal and drink or smoke pot socially is a lament for people struggling with addiction. "Everyone else is drinking and doing drugs, so why can't I do the same? I want to be like a normal person," clients say. It takes a long time for people to come to terms with the fact that they cannot use or they will be back in the same situation that they were in before, or worse.

---

5. https://www.cdc.gov/drugoverdose/data/statedeaths.html

The definition of addiction is a habit craving obsession creating a dependency on something you cannot stop. Addicts tell themselves that tomorrow will be better and that they can use just one more time and control that one-time use, even though they have heard many times that if they pick up and use it may be the last time they ever do it.

Chapter 10

"They called Ryan's death an accidental overdose," my daughter says, as if that explains her friend's death and justifies the day Ryan used drugs and died. "No one gets up in the morning and says today is the day I'm going to die!" Jim is shouting. He lowers his voice, but responds to a familiar hand gesture of mine reminding him we are in a public place. It's 2014 and my daughter, Jim and I are in IHOP near the recovery house in Kensington where my daughter lives. My ex looks down at his plate filled with pancakes smeared in syrup and butter, coffee and eggs and whispers, "They always say someone's death by overdose was accidental. No one means to die, but it happens all the time. Everyone thinks they are invincible." He is hoping to impact our daughter.

"Ryan had eighteen months clean," my daughter says, defending her friend's death. "The problem was she moved back in with her parents and they don't know anything about recovery. They still drank in front of her!" She is rationalizing her friend's death as if Ryan's moving home and moving in with her parents was the reason she decided to pick up and shoot heroin into her veins. "Heroin laced with Fentanyl is what killed Ryan. Sadly, she was only thirty years old," I remind Jess. "You don't know what you're buying on the street. Heroin laced with unknown substances is what killed Ryan. Picking up and using drugs after eighteen months clean is what took Ryan's life away. Her body went into cardiac arrest. No one wakes up in the morning and says today I am going to die." I repeat Jim's words, praying that something will get through to our daughter, some words of wisdom will change her mind and make a difference, stopping the addiction that is putting her in danger, tearing our family apart, ruining her life. I'm wondering if our daughter will be able to hold on to her few fragile months of sobriety.

No words of wisdom or living with her parents or

on the streets could have stopped Ryan from picking up and using and dying after eighteen months clean. Nothing and no one. Ryan, who once told Jess, "I will never overdose and die on drugs." Ryan, the child who played in our backyard, ate dinner in front of the TV, played Super Mario Brothers and jammed with my daughter on the eight-hundred-dollar Gibson electric guitar. Ryan, a sweet, middle-class child who went to the same private school as Jess and received the same private school education that should have guaranteed neither Jess nor Ryan would ever turn to drugs or die from an overdose. The child who came to our house during Halloween dressed as Superwoman, the same innocent girl who died from an overdose when she was only thirty years old.

"Ryan's moving back home did make a difference," my daughter says, grieving her friend's death as well as trying to make sense as to why she cannot come home and live at the house she grew up in while she is still using drugs.

Chapter 11

"Hurry, Mom! Come get me!" Jess's voice sounds strained and tense on my cellphone. "You can't miss me. I crashed into the wall on I-95. There are two police cars here, right before the Bridge Street Exit off of 95, lights flashing. There are police everywhere. I was in an accident. I'm on 95, I skidded across three lanes. I'm not hurt and I didn't hit any other cars. The police are here and I need a ride to the methadone clinic. I have to get to the clinic! And Mom, I swear I wasn't using anything. They made me walk on a line to see if I was high. The police asked me why my eyes were dilated. I told them I was on methadone and I was scared because I had just slammed into a wall on I-95 and now I'm talking to a police officer. They asked me why I was so scared and I told them it was because I had to get to the methadone clinic before it closed. I guess they believed me."

"Are you hurt? Was anyone else involved in the accident?" I ask Jess. Four years into her addiction, she decided to go on methadone. She was headed to the clinic when she crashed into the wall on I-95.

"No one was hurt. Just hurry Mom, okay? I have to get to the methadone clinic. It closes at noon on Sunday. The accident scared me."

I felt the same way. Jess could have been arrested, killed or hurt in the accident, or she could have hurt someone else.

"How did the accident happen?" I ask her when I finally arrive, both of us now sitting in the car on I-95 surrounded by police cars, motorists whizzing by at 80 miles an hour, cop cars with red lights flashing lined up behind us.

"I got pushed off the road by a tractor trailer," Jess explains. "I was trying to get off at Bridge Street to get to the methadone clinic but I was cut off by a truck. I slammed on the brakes and I guess the brakes locked up or something. The car froze, went sideways and backwards as it crossed over two lanes and smashed into this wall."

"You're lucky to be alive. I'm glad no one was hurt."

"The police made me stand on one foot and walk on a line. They asked me why my eyes were dilated. I told them I was on the way to the Methadone clinic trying to get there before it closes. What time is it Mom? Do you have any water?"

"What did you tell the police?"

"I told them I was on Methadone. Do you have water Mom? I'm thirsty. What time is it?" Jess asks, distracted and disoriented.

"I have some water in the trunk." Popping the trunk, I walk to the back of the car and grab a bottle of water. I glance at the smashed Ford her father gave her two months ago thinking she was ready to handle the responsibility of a car.

"I think she can handle the used car," her dad had said. "All of the other children drove it so if it's all right with you, I'm going to give it to her." I reluctantly agreed, ignoring the intuitive nudge that said my daughter was not ready for a car. Her Subaru had been repossessed four years before, and all her savings were gone. Memories of her addiction, moving from one recovery house to the next. The fact that Jess was living in Kensington, Philadelphia's badlands, cycling from relapse to recovery back to relapse again told me she was not ready—but I ignored my intuition that shouted no. She would never be ready until she could buy her own car and pay for the insurance, the gas and other bills herself. But maybe my daughter should have her turn?

"That car still has life in it. She should be able to get two more years out of it. How about if we split the cost and give it to her?" Jess's dad asked. He too dismissed the gut reaction that said our daughter was not ready for another car.

"I don't feel great about giving her the car. It's only a few years since her car was repossessed," I say to Jim.

"All of the other kids used the car," he says. The Green Pickle, as the car was known, a 1995 Ford, was now smashed on the highway.

"Please, Mom. I would love to have a car," Jess begged. "It would be so much easier than taking the subway especially on those cold winter mornings when I have to be at the Methadone clinic before 8 am. Besides, it will be cheaper than taking an Uber." Having ignored my intuition, Jess and I are now surrounded by police cars. The Green Pickle is smashed against the wall on I-95, totaled, being hooked up to a city tow truck. Once again, all of Jess's material possessions are gone.

"They're writing you a ticket," I say, handing my daughter a bottle of Poland Spring water from the trunk of my car. "Here's the ticket," the police officer leans into the window and hands me the $400 dollar fine and instructions on where to go to get the totaled car out of the City Municipal lot.

"You will get instructions in the mail on how to pay the ticket. At the Municipal Lot the officers will let you know the additional fines for storing the car until it is picked up and taken away by you. Best to get the car towed to the junk yard as soon as you can. Costs can be as high as $100 a day for storage if you don't pick it up from the municipal lot as soon as you can."

Sitting in the car talking about the accident, Jess professing her innocence, I later learn everything she said was a lie—Jess had been using and would have failed a drug test. Fortunately she was not given one, or she would have gone to jail. After the accident, on to the Methadone clinic, Jess and I spend the day at the

City Municipal parking lot getting the wrecked car out of Impoundment, towing it back to the mechanic near the house. "Too much damage," the mechanic says. A few days later the fines come in the mail. The total cost for the relapse, another $3,000. Jess is alive and no one is hurt—one of many miracles—but once again all of Jess's possessions are gone.

Chapter 12

"I'm telling you she relapsed," her father said at a family dinner a few weeks before the I-95 accident. "I found a crack pipe in her pocket. When I confronted her she said it wasn't her pipe. She's lying, Raven. Why would she have a crack pipe in her pocket if she hasn't relapsed? I don't want her at my house if she's using drugs. I don't want her around the other kids. I don't care that she's on methadone and that it's lifesaving, as you say. She's both using methadone and abusing street drugs. Methadone can be abused too. It's a life-saver medication if a person is ready to recover. She relapsed. I know the signs. Believe me Raven, I know the signs."

"We can't leave the family dinner. Besides I believe her when she tells me she is sober. I know she didn't relapse. She told me she didn't relapse and I believe her. She doesn't do crack," I say, defending Jess, certain my daughter always told me the truth.

"I swear up and down and even on Bruce," Jess had said, swearing on the life of her beloved dog. But her father was right. Even on methadone, Jess had relapsed and a few weeks later she had almost killed herself on Route I-95.

When I answered the cellphone and picked Jess up, I knew she was in serious trouble and could have been killed. At the time, she had been working as a shift supervisor at a local store. I believed Jess had finally gotten a handle on the most pressing issue of her life, her addiction. I believed she had turned a corner and was going to be all right—but in reality it was all wishful thinking and denial. The desire for the addiction nightmare to end made me "relapse" into denial and wishful thinking, my destructive psychological process. The addiction was finally over, I told myself. She was working, holding a steady job. But there is no "end" to the disease, there is only a one day at a time recovery. For families living the nightmare, addiction is a disease of denial that everything will get better just by hoping it will.

Chapter 13

Jeeps with Delaware and New Jersey license plates, men and women dressed in new suits drive across the Benjamin Franklin Bridge over the Delaware River Bridge to Kensington, a neighborhood where they can buy heroin and bring it back to their communities to sell. The drugs are laced with poisons sold to unsuspecting people who trust the drug dealer. Heroin sold to rich and poor alike. Addiction spreads unchecked. In Kensington, ground zero for opioid abuse, addicted mothers nod-out under the Market Frankford Street subway line; needles hang out of their arms, babies fall to the ground.

"There's quite a cast of characters living in Kensington," Jess says, knowing she has to find a way to cope and to survive. Her new home is Trinity, a recovery house in Kensington. We will not take her home. Jess takes us on a tour of Kensington, her new home.

"That guy over there on the corner with the sign that says 'Homeless' is begging for money to keep his heroin habit going," says Jess. She points to a thirty-year-old with baggy jeans and a long beard to his navel. "That guy did jail time, but he's panhandling back on the streets to keep his habit going." A young man bobs, weaves and leans against a lamppost, sliding slowly down to the pavement. Children stop riding their bikes to point and laugh. The addict, feet splayed, falls to the ground. "See that woman with the flaming red hair? She's twenty years old, a prostitute. She works the streets to keep her heroin habit going." My daughter is living in Kensington with a new cast of characters, including bed bugs, at Trinity House. But she is alive.

"When you get to Trinity House the people in charge make you run everything through a hot dryer for an hour to kill the bed bugs," Jess says. "You get undressed in front of the dryer or you won't be admitted to the Recovery House or get a bed to sleep in. You strip down to your skivvies and jump into the shower; clothing is dumped into the washing machine. Everything goes into the dryer. The bed bugs are killed by the heat. I got bit last night." A soldier in battle, Jess shows off the raised red welt bites and bruises from the nasty critters she now shares her bed with at night.

A few months later

"I'm ready to leave Trinity Recovery House and go out on my own. I saw an apartment in South Philadelphia. I can get a job at Shoprite."

"Do you feel like you have your addiction under control?" I naïvely ask.

"I do! I can work and take care of my money. I am getting better, Mom," Jess pleads. "All I need from you is the first and last month's rent and a security deposit. I'll carry the rest on my own. I promise," and I believe her. Two months later she is back on the streets, busted for buying heroin, sentenced to community service in Kensington where she was arrested.

"In order to get my record expunged, the Judge says I have to do my community service in Kensington.

I was arrested in Kensington, so I have to do community service in Kensington." She hands me a list of community organizations that will help. "We can call in the morning," she says. "*You* can call in the morning," I tell my daughter, wanting her to take charge of her life.

Chapter 14

"I left messages with many organizations on the list the Judge gave me to do community service, but no one called me back," Jess tells me.

"The courts should update the lists. Why didn't they call you back?" I ask Jess as she searches for a place to fulfill the community service. A friendly pat on the back from the judge and the words the judge said were, "See this as a new start. You have a two-week window to complete your community service." She was handed an outdated list of organizations to help her complete her community service. It was Rock Ministry in Kensington that answered her phone call and helped her meet the timeline, giving her the job of mopping floors and cleaning toilets at the church.

"What do people do if they can't get a ride to the area they were busted in to fulfill the legal requirement for community service?" her father asks.

"This is where they get stuck in the system," I tell Jim. "Completing community service is difficult for some people. They can't get a ride to the place where they were busted, don't have money or transportation to get there, and are still using drugs. A warrant is put out for their arrest. Eventually they get picked up by the police and go to jail. It's a vicious cycle." Jim is watching the painful nightmare of his daughter's addiction unfold. Every day for three weeks, and before Jess moves, once again, back to Trinity Recovery House, I drive her from South Philadelphia to Kensington so she can fulfill her community service mopping floors and cleaning toilets at the church. Rock Ministry and Buddy Pastor, the minister who oversees the activities at the church in Kensington, have a special place in my heart.

"See this as an opportunity to start your life over again," the judge had said to Jess. Rock Ministry was the only organization that had called Jess back from the list of dozens of places so she could fulfill the legal requirement of community service. She was able to complete the legal mandate without getting caught in the system and face jail time. And I could drive her from South Philadelphia to Kensington every day. She was too weak from using to organize her thinking and get herself to Kensington, and there would be many more attempts at recovery leading to relapse, disappointment and near arrests.

A few weeks later, she moves back to Trinity House. One night, the cellphone rings.

"Someone poured water on my bed blanket and sheets. I'm standing outside of Trinity a few blocks up the street on Kensington Avenue. I know I just got here but I'm not going back!"

"I'll pick you up, but only for tonight. Tomorrow you have to get on the phone and find a place to stay in another Recovery House or Sober Living House or go back to Trinity House. You can't come home while you are still using and I am not paying for another apartment like I did in South Philadelphia."

At eight o'clock at night Jess is standing on the corner of 3300 Kensington Avenue with four black trash bags stuffed with dirty clothing and bed bugs. "Thanks Mom," she says, as I open the trunk of the car. She puts the trash bags inside and closes the trunk. I drive her to a downtown center city hotel room for the night, pay for the hotel and say, "Stay in that room. Don't touch anything. Don't leave the hotel room. And don't relapse." I hope she will follow my orders. "If you don't want to go back to Trinity, then tomorrow you will have to find a new recovery house that takes your insurance. You figure it out. You do the work."

Chapter 15

"Will you come to Rock Ministries in Kensington with me, Mom? Pastor Buddy is great. He's in charge. A lot of recovery houses mandate people to attend Sunday Worship Service at Rock Ministry. Buddy said we should invite our family and I am inviting you!" Jess found a new recovery house in Frankford near Kensington with a mandate to attend Sunday Worship services at Rock Ministries at 2755 Kensington Avenue, where a sign with the words "Rock Ministries" hangs above the door. The locals affectionately call the church "The Rock." Christmas services will begin soon. "Are you nervous Mom?" Jess asks as she saunters over to the car parked across from Rock Ministries.

"A little, but I'm looking forward to seeing what this is all about," I say, locking the car and walking with Jess across the street to the chapel.

December 25, 2017. Rock Ministry is packed celebrating Christmas Day. Many parishioners struggling with addiction hope they can be saved by embracing their faith, ending the cycle of destruction and despair. A five-piece rock band stands on stage behind Pastor Buddy. Families from the neighborhood, along with men and women from dozens of recovery houses in Kensington and Frankford, are seated in wooden pews waiting for Pastor Buddy to speak, hoping he can help them recover from the nightmare of addiction.

Raised in Kensington, Pastor Buddy spent five years in a federal prison. His sentence was commuted, his time reduced for good behavior. Pastor Buddy was released back to the streets of Kensington a changed man. His faith grew. He had found his Savior and returned to Kensington to spread the Word, the message of The Gospel of Jesus Christ.

"Let's sit with your group from the Recovery House," I suggest, but Jess points to empty pew seats on the other side of the church away from the women she

A BLEARY-EYED STRANGER

now lives with. Pastor Buddy is standing on the raised platform in front of the congregants. "Give yourself over to Christ and be born again," he preaches to the neighborhood crowd, families dressed in their Sunday best. "If you want to be saved, come down to the front and stand next to the stage." Hesitantly, a group of men and women wearing torn coats and shoes without laces walk to the front of the stage and form a line in front of Pastor Buddy. Heads are bowed.

"Who wants to be saved by our Lord and Savior Jesus Christ?" Pastor Buddy's church rock band walk off the stage and into the crowd of worshippers, encouraging others to come to the front of the chapel and be saved. "Bring the Word of Jesus Christ into your hearts and be saved. Free yourself from addiction. Embrace The Word and Jesus Christ as your savior and you will be saved. Bring the Son of God into your heart. Redemption is here. God is forgiving. The Holy Spirit is healing. Turn your life over to Jesus Christ and be saved!" Men and women walk to the front of the stage and move closer to Pastor Buddy. Pastor Buddy, a jovial, round-faced man, walks off the stage and stands in front of each person. He gently places his hand on top of the bowed heads and begins his blessings. The men and women hope that by embracing the Word of God, they will be saved and have a new, successful life like Pastor Buddy.

"You are born again in Jesus Christ. Your soul is free from the demons of addiction that keep your soul a prisoner. Repeat after me and say, "I am born again in Jesus Christ. My soul is free from addiction and the demons that hold me captive."

"I am born again in Jesus Christ. My soul is free from the addiction and the demons that hold my soul captive," a choir of people wanting to be saved repeat.

"I am born again in Jesus Christ. My soul is free from the addiction and the demons that hold me captive. As I embrace the Word of Jesus Christ Son of God, I am saved," Pastor Buddy intones.

"I was once where you are, stealing, lying, living on the streets. At Christmas, I stole a Christmas tree for my family. I lied. I cheated. I used drugs. I was in prison for five years. I know what you are going through. You can live a different life and you can be saved. I was sentenced to eight years in prison and I served five. Five years of my life behind bars. Now I am married. I have a family and Rock Ministries is thriving. I turned my life over to the Lord Jesus Christ the Son of God who died for our sins. When I understood that I was saved, I began to heal my heart and my spirit. Now I started Rock Ministry. When you take the Lord Jesus Christ into your heart you too can be saved. God has given me many blessings. I am blessed and you are too. Can you say, "I take the Lord Jesus Christ into my heart and I am saved."

"I take the Lord Jesus Christ into my heart and I am saved," the group of men and women standing in front of the stage repeat.

"Every day I thank God for what he has given me, a beautiful wife and children. A growing ministry that is helping others live better lives. Every day I pray and remember that it is by God's grace that I am free from my demons and the past behaviors that kept me on the streets using drugs. I am grateful. I follow the Word the Gospel of Jesus Christ our Lord and Savior, the one and only Son of God who sacrificed and died for our sins so that we can be born again into eternal life. Did you know that Jesus Christ died for us, suffered for us, and we don't have to suffer anymore? Did you know that once you are saved you don't have to suffer? If you believe in what I am saying, say Amen."

"Amen," a chorus of men and women whisper, heads bowed.

"Through the power of grace and the Holy Spirit spiritual riches are in my life and can be yours, too. Take the Word of Jesus Christ, the son of God, into your heart and you will be saved."

"Do you accept Jesus Christ as your Lord and Savior?" Pastor Buddy places his hand on the heads of the men and women wishing to be saved and freed from addiction. Standing next to a giant of a man who conquered his struggles and created a life filled with success and service to the community, hope floods the Rock Ministry Calvary Chapel. Heads nod and say Amen.

Chapter 16

"Do you want to hurt yourself?" Five months later, after Christmas day at "The Rock," Jess has relapsed and is in the hospital. The nurse at Aria Bucks Hospital in Frankford Philadelphia leans over my daughter, who is curled up in a fetal position. She places three fingers on Jess's wrist and checks her pulse.

"Do you have a suicide plan to hurt yourself?" Jess is unresponsive.

"Sweetheart, please answer the nurse. Do you want to hurt yourself?"

"Yes, I want to die," she says. "I can't take it anymore. I can't stop using drugs. I try and stop. For a short time it works, and then someone comes up to me on the streets and offers me drugs. I don't have the willpower to turn them down. Even parents of my friends are using drugs. I know that's no excuse, but I can't walk away. I can't say no. What the hell is wrong with me? I am weak." She curls into a ball. The nurse leans over my daughter and presses the call button above the bed.

"Calling for transport to Friend's Psychiatric Hospital." The nurse is requesting an ambulance for my daughter. "We need transport to Friends Psychiatric Hospital right away."

"Where are they sending me?" Jess whispers.

"The ambulance will be here soon. It will take you to Friend's Hospital, a psychiatric hospital," the nurse says. Founded in 1813 by Quakers, in the 1800s Friends Hospital was an "asylum for people deprived of the use of their reason"—an accurate description of what is going on with Jess. Her loss of reason brought on by drug use—heroin and benzodiazepines—has taken away her ability to think coherently. After Friends Hospital, Jess will be admitted to Kirkbride mental hospital. Jess's "bottom" has been reached with delirium, confusion, disorientation and hallucinations brought on by drugs. Kirkbride, a mental hospital that houses people struggling with addiction and mental illness named after Thomas Kirkbride, was founded in 1841. At the time, the place was designed to create better treatment plans and outcomes for people struggling with mental illness. Hopefully they will be able to help my daughter.

"Can I ride with her to Friend's Hospital?" I ask the nursing staff.

"That's against insurance regulations. It's best if you meet her there. Here's the address, 4641 E. Roosevelt Boulevard." The evening shift nurse writes it down on a yellow sticky pad and hands it to me.

"Will she get better?" I ask the nurse, who averts her eyes and says, "She has to try harder."

It's a disease and she is trying, I silently defend.

"I have to go home and feed the dogs," I whisper to Jess. "I'll try and meet you at Friend's Hospital in a few hours." I reach for my daughter, stroking her arm. Her eyes are shut; she is curled up in a ball, drifting in and out of sleep. Her emaciated body is transferred from the emergency room hospital bed to the ambulance where my daughter is strapped down with thick brown leather straps. Lights blinking, sirens wailing,

Jess is transported to Friend's Hospital in Northeast Philadelphia.

A few hours later she calls me.

"Mom, they won't admit me to Friends Hospital. I told them I want to hurt myself like everyone told me to say, but they won't admit me. I don't think they believe me. I'm so tired. Help me, Mom. I don't know what to do. I've been yelling and telling them I need help. I'm depressed but they won't let me in. I've been wandering around the grounds talking to the wild animals, the deer, possums and raccoons. I can communicate with them! Did you know that all you have to do is look directly into the animal's eyes and listen to their message to hear what they are saying? I crouch down on the ground real low and get quiet. The animals come up to me and send me messages. They tell me they love me, Mom. Can you imagine? They can talk!"

"You're walking around the grounds at Friends Hospital instead of trying to get into the hospital?" I ask, exasperated with Jess.

"I told you, they won't let me in. I don't have any money to get the bus and go anywhere so I walked around the grounds. It's quiet this early in the morning.

The deer stare at me and whisper, "There is only love." Only love, Mom. I don't have to do drugs. I can communicate with animals and get high. Did you know that animals can communicate messages to you? I talk to the possum and other animals, but I can't get into Friends Hospital. Everyone told me what to say to get admitted. I do want to hurt myself but they turned me away. Do you think it's because I've been here so many times before? They probably don't believe I'm depressed. They think I'm high and they don't want to deal with drug addicts. Probably my insurance won't pay. They gave me a cab voucher back to center city Philadelphia, but I want to come home. Will you come pick me up? Please Mom. You said you were coming up here to help me. Are you? I feel sick Mom, really sick. I swear to you I haven't used any drugs but I can't think straight. Something is happening to me and I am scared, really scared shitless."

"What the hell is Friends Hospital talking about when they say they won't let you in?" I say, infuriated with the insurance company, sorting through Jess's lies.

"Jess, it's almost 5:00 a.m. It's morning. Take a cab to the Northeast Treatment Center, the NET, the methadone clinic, and get dosed with methadone."

"Mom, the NET doesn't open till 8:30 a.m. I don't know if they will dose me if I relapsed. What am I supposed to do until then? Can't I come home? I'm hungry and tired and I need a shower."

Chapter 17

"Keep her off the streets!" A new edict from her father, a frantic text. Several hours later Jess is home curled up next to the dryer asleep on the floor. When she wakes up she wraps herself in a blanket and walks around the house naked.

"Thanks for picking me up Mom. When I was on the streets, I went to someone's house looking for a place to sleep and eat. I didn't know what I was doing, I was out of my mind delirious and sick and so scared Mom, so very scared. When I look in the mirror I don't recognize myself." She touches the black circles under her eyes, hollow cheeks receding into her face. "I'm having a mental breakdown, Mom."

"You can't abruptly stop using drugs. You went into withdrawal. Did you know you could have had seizures? Getting off drugs or alcohol requires a medical detoxification, otherwise you can make yourself so sick that you don't recover and you could die." Another lecture from her mother, hoping the facts about addiction might save my daughter's life. "No wonder your speech was slurred and you were sweating, your memory gone, anxiety soaring through the roof. You are having withdrawal symptoms from benzodiazepines, a class of drugs known as tranquilizers. That's the last thing you want to do to your mind and body. It adds to the anxiety and depression you already struggle with." I'm thinking about Jess's undiagnosed depression, a disease she has had since high school. During her next to last year in college, after her grandfather died, she was overwhelmed with grief; it was a dark time when she could no longer cope with the stress in her life. She dropped out of college and returned a year later to finish and earn a degree in business, her depression not addressed with therapy and anti-depressants.

"You can't stay here at the house and detoxify. You need to go to a hospital for a medical detoxification before things get worse." Jess is wrapped in a blanket next to the dryer, hugging Bruce, staring wide-eyed into the cat's eyes.

"Talk to me Brucie dog. Tell me how you feel. I love you B. Dog. I will always love you. You would never leave me, would you?" The dog wiggles out of her arms.

"I have to go to work for a few hours," I tell Jess. "I'll be back soon. We'll figure out what to do and where you can go for help." I'm hesitant to leave her, hoping the house will be in one piece when I return. I'm praying she will stay inside and not wander the neighborhood with the grey fleece blanket wrapped around her naked body.

"Do you have to go to work? Please don't leave. I can't be alone." Jess gathers the blanket over her head and pulls it into a makeshift hoodie over her eyes. My thirty-seven-year-old daughter climbs into my bed.

"I don't know what's happening to me. Where am I?" She asks, getting out of bed, roaming from room to room. "I wanted to stop using so I just stopped. I swear I'm not using drugs. But something bad is happening to me."

"Get dressed. We're going over to Einstein Crisis Response Center," I say, calling work to tell them I'd be late. "Emergency at home," I leave a message for the supervisor. "Let's go," I say to Jess, searching for car keys, locking up the house. Einstein Crisis Response Center will do a psychiatric evaluation and find a recovery house and perhaps a facility for a medically assisted detox.

Chapter 18

"She's not telling you the truth," the crisis center intake worker at Einstein says.

"What do you mean she's not telling me the truth? If my daughter says she stopped using drugs then she stopped using drugs! I believe her!" I say, irate that someone doubts my daughter.

"Go home and come back on Monday," the crisis worker says. "It's Friday. We don't have any beds. We are in an opioid epidemic crisis in Philadelphia. We don't have beds and there is nothing we can do for your daughter right now until a bed opens up. You can stay in the waiting room and rest in the chairs. A bed may open up on Monday, at least I hope so. Come back on Monday. Something will open up. It always does on Monday morning, although empty beds get filled quickly."

"What do you mean you hope? Are you telling me that there is not one bed in the entire city of Philadelphia for my daughter to sleep in over the weekend?" I ask, hoping they can find a place for Jess to sleep, afraid I won't be able to handle what is coming if Jess is home for the weekend.

"She will come out of it," my best friend, a psychiatric nurse, reassures me. "I've seen it many times on the psych floor in the hospital in Burlington, Vermont. Patients come into the hospital out of their minds. They don't know who they are or where they are. It's frightening to watch, especially the hallucinations and the paranoia that happens when people suddenly stop using drugs. Like Jess, people think they can communicate with animals or they want to hurt themselves to avoid the pain of withdrawal. Sometimes, and not to their benefit, they sign themselves out of the hospital. They use drugs for relief from the symptoms of withdrawal. When they feel better, they readmit themselves into the hospital. The cycle repeats over and over again. All rational thinking is gone, which explains the reason Jess is curled up next to the dryer in a ball at home. She is withdrawing and needs medical help."

"On the psych floor patients say everyone is staring at me," my friend continues. "They say, 'Stop staring at me. You hate me, I know you hate me. You're trying to hurt me', they shout," She explains the paranoid behaviors of patients with substance abuse problems. "Paranoia sets in from the drugs and the withdrawal. Patients believe others are talking about them behind their back. They frantically paw the air, swatting away invisible people, disembodied faces floating around. They scream at things we can't see. Paranoia and bizarre behaviors come with the territory of abusing street drugs. It's called a substance-induced psychosis, a break from reality. What people don't know is that people can have a psychotic break from reality, a psychosis, from smoking marijuana. People can hallucinate from smoking pot. With continued use, psychiatric problems can become more serious even with marijuana. It's similar to a person with dementia. They don't know that they are hallucinating. Everything seems real to them. Reality and fantasy gets confused, mixed up in their minds. At the hospital, we treat them with medications that can help them relax and stop the hallucinations. A few days later, when they are feeling better, they apologize for their behavior. We have a lot of repeat patients. "Frequent flyers," we call them. Drug addiction is hard to control."

Drugs are made of chemicals, many similar to the chemicals in our system. Drugs alter the way nerve cells normally send, receive, and process information. They do this by (1) imitating the brain's natural chemical messengers, (2) by over-stimulating the "reward circuit" of the brain with excess chemicals, and (3) binding to the receptors in the brain. For example, some drugs such as marijuana and heroin have a similar structure to chemical messengers called neurotransmitters, which are naturally produced by the brain. Because of this similarity, these drugs are able to "fool" the brain's receptors and activate nerve cells into sending abnormal messages. This results in the high you feel when you take these drugs.[6]

"Was I really that crazy and out of it?" Patients ask when they come out of the delirium. "Jess will be okay," my friend reassures me, trying to put my mind at ease, but I am not convinced. I have never seen Jess

---

6. https://www.phoenixhouse.org/faq/what-happens-to-your-brain-when-you-take-drugs/

like this. Has she destroyed her mind forever?

"I have never seen Jess behave like this," I tell my friend. "She is a mess, wandering around the house walking aimlessly from room to room. She says she can talk to animals. She is curled up in a fetal position next to the dryer, holding on to it for warmth and comfort. She said she was cold and then she got into my bed, curled up, and except for a blanket wrapped around, she is naked."

"Can I sleep in your bed?" Jess asked, wrapping the blanket tighter around her head. "Move over there," I say pointing to the floor in front of the bedroom door. "Here's your sleeping blanket. Put it on the floor and use it as a mat. Cover yourself with your blanket. Try to rest, please Jess, calm down and rest. You heard the crisis worker at Einstein Crisis Response Center say there are no open beds in hospitals in Philadelphia. We are in an opioid crisis. The crisis worker is hoping there will be a bed open on Monday. We have two days together in the house to make this work. Your father is afraid for you and wants you off the streets. You have to stay here. The only way we can do this is if you calm down and rest. I have to get some sleep and go to work tomorrow. If you can't control the anxiety then let's go over to the emergency room at the hospital and see what they can do for you."

"I can't rest. I'm afraid. What will happen to me next? Have I lost my mind forever?"

Chapter 19

On Monday morning Jess and I return to Einstein Crisis Response Center. "A bed has opened up at Kirkbride, the psychiatric hospital at 48th and Haverford Ave in Philadelphia. Go to this address. The admissions department will have her paperwork and they will sign her in," the Intake crisis worker at Einstein Crisis Response Center says, filling out paperwork and faxing it over to Kirkbridge and handing me the address. I drive Jess to Kirkbride, sign her in, and say goodbye.

"You will be safe here," I reassure my daughter, hugging her. "I love you."

A week later, on visiting day, her father and I go

to Kirkbride to see our daughter. The entrance to the visiting center is a large gymnasium in the basement of the hospital. We wait with other families for Jess to be brought down from the locked units. Metal chairs are haphazardly placed around the gymnasium room; windows are covered in metal mesh that can't be opened. Dozens of people, chairs arranged in circles marking their family space, wait for loved ones.

"Kirkbride looks like the visiting room in a state correctional facility," I tell Jess when she takes a seat between her father and me. In lieu of serving time, people who have been busted for drugs are mandated to Kirkbride for rehabilitation. Families visit with loved ones and come to terms with the fact that recovery is a slow, tedious process, one that has repeatedly landed their loved ones in an institution. This time it is Kirkbride. The addiction cycle continues, a hamster on a wheel; hospital to jail and back to probation, which often gets violated, increasing the risk of chronic legal problems. Then back to the streets, coping with unmanageable additional legal and financial problems, unable to pay fines or find transportation to and from the place where they were arrested and mandated to do community service, a revolving wheel, relapse, recovery, relapse, streets and jail and sometimes death.

"You are one step away from jail!" I shout over the deafening noise in the gymnasium, fearful for Jess's life, and my ex and daughter nod in agreement. "You're lucky that schizophrenia doesn't run in our family. If it did there is a possibility you would not have come back from this last relapse, this "delirium," as the doctor at Kirkbride put it." Stating the facts helps me face the disease of addiction. Saying it straight keeps me out of denial.

"You were diagnosed with a delirium. Did you tell the doctor about your history with depression?" I ask, encouraging my daughter to take charge of her mental health and stop self-medicating with drugs from the street. My daughter is an addict. Jess is an addict. She has cravings for substances that are dangerous and could lead to death. "Accidental drug overdose is currently the leading cause of death in the United States for those under 50. Drug overdose deaths now exceed those attributable to firearms, car accidents, homicides, or HIV/AIDS. More Americans died from a drug overdose in 2017 alone than died in the entire Vietnam War."[7]

---

7. https://drugpolicy.org/issues/drug-overdose

Saying it straight to Jess helps me understand what happened to our daughter in her "delirium," and how in four years the disease brought her so low, our family torn apart, Jess in a mental institution where most people are mandated by the courts to stay and recover. Jess's roommates are people who have been in prison for dealing and using drugs.

During Jess's delirium she asked, "Where am I? I lost my things. All my stuff! My bags got heavy. I put them down somewhere, I think in the lobby of a hotel," she said when she called while aimlessly walking around downtown Philly near her apartment on Spring Garden Streets. A backpack filled with clothing, a toothbrush, cigarettes, bottled water and her cellphone were left in the lobby of a company, later found and returned by the CEO of the company.

"What was she doing in this part of town?" said the CEO who was kind enough to call Jess's father whose number was in the cellphone and return the lost bag to Jess. "Does she live downtown?"

"Visiting friends." Another lie to a stranger, people who would not understand the struggle of addiction, people who would judge addiction, judge my daughter and say *She could stop using if she wanted to. She just has to exert self-control. She is an addict. What can you expect? Addicts steal, lie and cheat. If they tried harder they could control what's going on and stop using drugs. Picking up and using is a choice. Every time they pick up it is a choice, knowing nothing about the disease, the cravings, the hijacking of the brain.*

"What are you thinking?" I ask Jess's father on the ride home from Kirkbride.

"We have stuck by her, bought her food, paid for cigarettes, given her subway tokens. We picked her up and drove her to the next recovery house when she wore out her welcome in the old one. Soon she was back on the streets with more hospital emergency room visits. One night you were brave enough to leave her on the streets in Kensington hoping for the best, praying she would figure it out for herself. When she saw how serious you were she called a friend and lived with that friend for several months. Shortly after that she was arrested for buying heroin in Kensington and spent the night in jail. If she hadn't had us to pay her fines and you to drive her to her community service she'd be in jail and released back to the streets in Kensington. We talked, we texted, we visited, telling her we loved her. We never stopped loving her, but we cannot do the hard work of keeping her from picking up and using drugs and relapsing again." Jim is disheartened at the slow progress of recovery.

"Relapse is part of recovery," I gently remind him.

"I know," her father says, ending the conversation, remembering the number of times during our marriage he relapsed before recovering at Fairmont Hospital forty years ago.

"The lifestyle can be addicting too," I tell him, thinking about clients who said they can make thousands of dollars in a day selling drugs on the streets. With easy money people can buy a car and have access to an apartment and women who want to be with a man with money, never mind he's a drug addict. "It's an addicting lifestyle not only because of the money but the opportunity to be entrepreneurial, to have an identity, and be somebody in the neighborhood. There is a natural high in making deals," I tell my ex, who is now a successful businessman. "Of course there is the risk of a deal gone bad, a drug dealer or someone getting shot and killed. Caught up in the excitement of wheeling and dealing, people don't think about the risk of going to jail, sometimes for a lifetime, or dying, and only think of the high of living in the fast lane and making a fast buck, even though getting hurt or killed is part of the territory of dealing drugs."

"Raven, it's sad that our daughter is in Kirkbride with people who, like herself, have drug addiction and mental illness. For so many years we minimized Jess's depression. Addiction is not anybody's dream for their child. Kirkbride looks like a prison."

"Did you know when Kirkbride was founded in the 1800's it was designed to set a new precedent in the field of mental health?" I tell Jim. "It doesn't look like it, but a century ago, Kirkbride was considered a state-of-the-art mental health facility. Other mental institutions around the country were over-crowded and filthy. Over a hundred years ago residents were chained to their beds with little if any mental health treatment. Residents struggling with mental illness with minimal treatment lived in squalor. Hard to believe that a little over a hundred years ago, Kirkbride was a trend setter in cleanliness in contrast to other asylums, as they were called back then."

"By the looks of it, Kirkbride hasn't changed much," Jess's father says. "It's depressing. I wish we could wave a magic wand and have her stop using drugs. It's up to her. There is nothing we can do but love and support her. Right now she is in a downward slide. Maybe this previous state-of-the-art facility can turn her around. Maybe Kirkbride will be her bottom."

Jim is frightened and tired of dealing with Jess's addiction, relapse after relapse, emergency rooms, inpatient and outpatient, intensive outpatient, (IOP) Medication Assisted Treatment (MAT) and Suboxone treatments, the latter my ex, who is old school recovery, considers still using drugs. "It's Jess's process. We are there for her, but she has to do the hard work and want to recover. She has to learn that she is powerless over drugs and alcohol and that she cannot manage her emotions by eating pills or smoking pot to make her stress go away," Jim says. "No matter what you do for an addict they don't appreciate or benefit from it. She has to want recovery. She has to do it herself. I recovered when I understood that I was powerless over alcohol and drugs. I'd be back at the beginning on Brown and Wallace Streets if I ever picked up again. I'd lose everything, just like she did if I relapsed, and like I did with you and Jess. Jess must learn she can never use again. At some point she is going to have to come off methadone. Keep in mind Raven, people can abuse methadone too." Her father does not understand the benefits of medication-assisted treatment (MAT) to ease the struggle and change behaviors related to addiction. "Medication-assisted treatment is still using drugs," Jess's father says, getting out of the car, leaning back into the window. "Maybe I have to start thinking differently about methadone. In my day, you did it cold turkey. I'm an old-timer, I guess."

"Methadone is life-saving, better than self-medicating on the streets," I say, trying to convince him of the benefits of this life-saving treatment. "People can abuse methadone but if administered correctly, and with a person's commitment to recovery, it can save their lives too. Methadone reduces cravings and withdrawal symptoms. With medical supervision and periodic urine screenings, staff at the methadone clinic monitors a person making sure they are not abusing methadone. Urine screenings can detect if a client is using other substances while getting methadone treatment. During that time, no matter how long it takes, a person on methadone can rebuild their life and not be subject to HIV, hepatitis and a life of crime on the streets. Medication-assisted treatments (MAT) helps calm the addicted brain. This gives a person the opportunity to change behaviors," I tell Jim.

"Why don't you just stop using drugs?" I once asked Jess. "That was before I understood the benefits of methadone and other medicine-assisted treatments like Suboxone to help her stop using," I tell my ex-husband.

"What was her response?" Jim asked.

She said, "addiction doesn't work like that." She explained that a normal person can have just one drink or share a joint, but she can't do that. She said, "I always want more and more, hard for you to understand Mom because you don't have the disease of addiction. If you go to a party and have a glass of wine or two that is probably satisfying and enough for you. If you find yourself feeling woozy or out of control you stop drinking. I cannot do that. I can't use willpower and just stop using. My brain doesn't work like that. I always crave more. Addiction runs in my genes. Daddy had addiction problems. His siblings my aunt and uncles and daddy's father my grandfather all struggled with drugs and alcohol. That should tell you something, Mom. Stop blaming yourself. I was destined to become an addict."

Chapter 20

In 2013, when I first learned about my daughter's addiction, at Jim's suggestion, I began attending Al-Anon meetings. "Hang on to the moon," the facilitator began at the Al-Anon 12-step beginners meeting for families with loved ones struggling with addiction. During those first years when I did not know where to turn or what to do to help save my daughter's life, I hung on to the facilitator's words: "hang on to something, hang on to the moon." They gave me hope. I could get through another day. "Keep coming back," the meeting participants said in unison.

Living in fear, desperate for answers, I kept going back. My child was in serious danger and there was nothing I could do about it. Jess was slipping away, caught in the cycle of addiction, unrecognizable to me.

I could not reach her. She was in the beginning stages of learning about addiction, believing that by sheer force of will power she could stop using. She did not want to be an addict but it was hard for her to embrace Step 1 of the 12-step program that she was powerless—and as I was learning in Al-Anon, so was I.

"Hang on to anything, hang on to the moon," the Al-Anon group facilitator said, giving me the strength to go to work, come home to an empty house and get up the next day to do it all over again. Hanging on is all I could do as I went day after day, week after week to Al-Anon meetings, sometimes four times a week dealing with grief and loss of control. In the Al-Anon meetings I was certain I would find the secret that would stop the train wreck bearing down on our family. I went to meetings for fellowship, wisdom, strength, and the message that I hadn't caused her addiction, that I couldn't control it, or cure it. Slowly I came out of denial and began to understand that Jess has her own spiritual path, the disease of addiction as a part of that path, my Al-Anon recovery was my path. Jess would have to find her way back to sanity, as would I with the help of my higher power.

In the beginning in Al-Anon, I blamed myself for my daughter's addiction. I was her mother and should have seen it coming. It would take many years to come to understand that I had not caused her disease of addiction, and I could not control it or cure it—words that are repeated often in Al-Anon meetings. She alone was the only person who could recover from her addiction, a slow, long process. In the meetings I asked questions like how had I contributed to her addiction? As my recovery in Al-Anon grew stronger I understood that I did not cause her addiction, couldn't cure it, and definitely could not control it. Pre-Al-Anon days, I believed that I had control over the direction of my daughter's life and that I had the power to help direct her life path. Wasn't she like me? She came to my meditation workshops. She was exposed to ideas of higher consciousness, meditation, yoga and organic food, and since there were no drugs or alcohol in our home, she would be spared from the disease of addiction. I was wrong. In Al-Anon I discovered I could not directly help her. There was nothing I could do to stop the hijacking of the brain that produces cravings and the subsequent relapsing from addiction. I had to focus on my own recovery and take care of myself.

Recovery in Al-Anon puts the focus back on oneself, strengthening one's connection to a higher power. Setting emotional boundaries was at the top of the list with my daughter. When I came into Al-Anon I thought I could change her. I did not know that I had emotional and spiritual work to do on myself. My higher power was strong, or so I believed—but it too often consisted of my telling the God of my understanding what the outcome of an event should look like. I was still controlling events. In the process of recovery, my relationship and my understanding of a higher power deepened. I gained spiritual insight, and had what is called in Al-Anon a spiritual awakening—no flashing golden lights but a lovely expansion of consciousness. Compassion for myself and others, and faith in my higher power increased and anger and resentments lessened. My heart opened and I was less afraid.

At the 12-step Al-Anon meeting, folded index cards placed on the table and around the room impart Al-Anon wisdom: "Listen and Learn," "Easy Does It," "Keep it Simple," "Live and Let Live," "FEAR – False Evidence Appearing Real." The fear I was living with was not false and the evidence was real. My daughter was an opioid addict living in Kensington. I was in the Al-Anon meetings, far from home, listening to and hanging on to the experience strength and hope of others, eyes closed and tears ready to fall, wondering where I failed my daughter, believing I must have caused her addiction and had the power to cure it. Learning that addiction is a family disease; her grandfather, aunts and uncles and father all struggle with the disease of addiction, all in recovery and doing well. An Al-Anon slogan, "Listen and Learn," reminds me to suspend judgment, come out of denial and let go of the fantasy that by attending Al-Anon meetings I can cure my daughter's addiction. *Jess will see me trying hard, attending Al-Anon meetings and the love we have for each other will make her try harder and conquer her addiction.* By attending Al-Anon meetings I can influence the outcome of events in her life and control her addiction. The strong will that brought me into adulthood sober and determined to live life to the fullest is strong enough for both of us and will control her addiction. My love for her, a mother's love and my strong will for my daughter is stronger than God's will or at least God will have mercy on our family and keep the both of us alive while she heals her addiction.

In Al-Anon meetings four times a week far from home, I was reminded that I couldn't control the outcome of events. I could only live my life and try to control the fear and worry that came with addiction focusing on myself.

I went to Al-Anon meetings to save my daughter's life and saved my own. I believed that the more meetings I went to the more she would benefit and heal. My going to Al-Anon meetings would impact her and she would stop using, but she did not. She continued to struggle with addiction, and it was getting worse. I could not save her or any human being from the disease of addiction. It took many years to stop blaming my daughter's addiction on my behaviors and what I did wrong raising her. Only the alcoholic or addict can change the addiction, and that, as I have heard so many people say including my daughter, happens by the grace of God. Her father was an addict, aunt's uncles and grandparents on her father's side of the family all had the disease of addiction and recovered, and she could too.

Al-Anon taught me that addiction is a disease with a genetic component. Before Al-Anon, I continued to blame myself. I should have been a stronger mother, better able to set boundaries. Perhaps things would have turned out differently. If I had been a mother willing to go to Al-Anon meetings as suggested by the social worker at the hospital in 1982 when Jess was three years old and her father went into Fairmount Hospital the beginning of his recovery, perhaps things might have been different for my daughter. Al-Anon meetings, a 12-step program for family and friends struggling with loved ones who have the disease of addiction, have taught me that Jess is her own person making decisions taking her down a path where she got caught in the cycle of addiction. There are always clues that a person is in a slide, but not all slides lead to addiction. Many children grow up in horrific situations and never turn to drugs or alcohol to self-medicate their pain away. Of course many do, but I'm a psychotherapist. I look for reasons why. I need to know what happened to Jess and why addiction is so difficult to recover from. I continue to explore the reasons and the difficulty of recovering from addiction, perhaps lessening self-blame. Addiction, a family disease, something she will have to struggle with and overcome on her own like her father, uncles and aunts before her; a disease I have no control over, and one I thought she would never have. "I am powerless," I repeat silently in the meeting, "and my life has become unmanageable." Thoughts of childhood float into my mind.

Chapter 21

My Story

It was 1952 and I was five years old. I was sitting in the middle of my family's living room on the floor playing with my dollhouse. My sister was there beside me on the Oriental rug. All of a sudden, as in a fairy tale, someone knocked at the front door. A special delivery package had just arrived in the mail from my father, for both my sister and me. My parents had divorced; my father was in Spain "on business," my mother told us. These mailed packages were a sign to me that he had not forgotten us and would soon be home so we could spend our Sundays together.

My sister ripped open her package, wrapping paper flying around the room. Daddy had sent her a red leather vest with shiny gold buttons. It took her only three seconds to unwrap her gift, then she took a deep breath, and with that familiar squint in her eye which usually signaled trouble for me, she said, sweetly, "Let me see what you have in there." I slowly peeled off the brown paper from around my present, wanting to savor each precious minute, keeping the memory of my father close to me for as long as I could. Eventually, a matador doll from Spain emerged, nestled in white tissue. I ran my fingers down his black, sequined pants, up and over his red jacket, and across his soft, black felt hat. Then I took the shiny silver sword from around his waist. For a brief moment I held him in my arms. Then I gave away my doll to my sister, as she had silently requested.

My sister is the first person, but by no means the last, in a long line of people I gave my possessions to. Hundreds of things: a blue Pontiac convertible, a trip to Jamaica, a closet full of fashionable clothes, my dog, even my bank account. Once I gave away my bicycle to a new boy neighbor down the street when he said that he had lost his.

Actually, there were so many giveaways I cannot even remember them all. Taking care of people at my own expense never mattered to me, as long as I was helping "a friend in need." Therefore, it was no surprise to anyone in my family when they heard I was going to graduate school to become a psychiatric social worker.

Over the years, I would eventually work for a hospice, in a soup kitchen, a shelter for runaways. I was the founder of a holistic health networking agency. I was the director of a family counseling agency specializing in runaway and homeless youth.

To all outward appearances, I was the quintessential professional, the one with her life on track. But in reality I empathize with a woman's pain when she tells me she spends her life taking care of her husband, cooking, cleaning for her children, and giving away things to her friends and neighbors. I know this woman, because this woman at one time was me. At age forty-five I discovered that I excessively gave to other people and often compulsively took care of them as well. I discovered the truth about myself as the result of marriage to a man I would have done anything for, my second marriage, to Jess's stepfather. I lived to make him happy. One day, he left a note stating he needed time alone, leaving my daughter and me to figure out what happened. It was a few months after Jess's Bat Mitzvah. She was thirteen years old. What went wrong?

One evening, as I was driving back from the supermarket with food from our favorite Saturday night Mexican dinner, I saw my second husband stopped at a traffic light. He was going in the opposite direction from our house. I waved and smiled my brightest smile and hung my head out the car window, yelling at him, all smiles and good cheer, wanting to discuss the note that said, "I need time alone."

"Pull over," I called. I waved him off to the side of the road and when he reluctantly parked, I climbed into his car beside him. That's when I saw his packed suitcase, tossed onto the back seat of the car, the one we had used the month before on the trip to Hawaii that I had financed on my MasterCard.

"I saw the note you left," I said.

"Take care," he said to me.

And that was the end. That's all he ever said. As he stared out the front windshield, his arms folded tightly over his chest, I smoothed the long hair of his braid, but he never once looked at me. After I got out of the car and drove home to my now empty house, I read the note again.

"I need time alone. Best regards."

It was as if someone had died in my arms. At night when I could not sleep, I paced the floor and when I finally slept, I dreamed that I was paralyzed and sprayed with a lethal chemical that controlled my mind and my body. In the dream, I was in great danger of dying. I had to make a decision as to whether I wanted to live or to die. In reality, however, I did not have a decision to make. I had only one choice: to keep going. I had a daughter to raise into adulthood.

A few weeks later, I dragged myself up a flight of stairs to my first 12-step recovery meeting, Co-dependents Anonymous. In this meeting, where I sat for three years with strangers who eventually became my friends, I took off my mask. For years I had worn the face of Superwoman, healer of all wounds, someone who gave away too much of herself. I felt feelings I had never felt before: a myriad sensations, including a new one: shame. This was the feeling I had buried so deeply from my conscious awareness that for all purposes, it did not even exist. By taking care of people and giving them my things, I avoided facing painful feelings, memories, and fears.

My deepest fear of all, of course, was abandonment. This I kept at bay. Instead I imagined that a good, beautiful, and benevolent fairy, like the one in Cinderella, would make all bad things disappear with a wave of her sparkling silver wand. I believed that she would always be there for me, as I was for others. Unlike my mother, who was always too busy to take care of me, my fairy godmother was the embodiment of perfect love—she was the perfect woman, and the person I was going to be.

I kept up this fantasy all through my childhood and into my twenties when I moved into an ashram to worship at the feet of gurus who naturally became my new fairy godmother. Now I gave all things to my guru, money as well as love and devotion. Of course, by now this was easy for me. I was a master at giving things away for connection and love.

I worshipped at the feet of a good many gurus, and I lived in one ashram after another seeking truth and fairy godmothers, yet I hated the politics of ashram life. My favorite ashram, the place where I lived the longest while attending graduate school at Tulane

University securing a degree in psychiatric social work in New Orleans Louisiana, was a Yogi Bhajan ashram called 3 HO, standing for Healthy Happy and Holy. Through the practice of Kundalini yoga, I was seeking a deeper connection to my higher power. All the while, I affirmed my love for everything. But I felt as if I was holding my breath hoping the pain from childhood would magically disappear. And like holding your breath, you can only do it for so long.

Then one night, with a nagging feeling that could not be washed away no matter how many hours I sat with my eyes closed or my legs tucked underneath me, I left the ashram for good. As a replacement, I took my fantasies into two marriages.

For the seven years of each marriage, and through several illnesses which I ignored, believing that God or some omnipotent force would save me, I kept on giving, and I kept on praying that a pain in my side from gastrointestinal issues would go away. But I ignored it and it landed me the hospital. Eventually I got better. But the pain in my heart from the ending of my second marriage would not go away. I missed my second husband and wanted to make the marriage work. I did not want a second divorce.

In Co-dependents Anonymous I began to feel a new set of feelings, and I was able to grieve, a word I did not think applied to me. To ease the ache in my heart from the loss of my second marriage and finding a note that read "I need time alone," from a man I loved, I went to meetings every day and walked for miles, while memories of people I had taken care of flooded my mind. And, I waited for this husband, in much the same way I had waited for my father to return from Spain as well as on Sundays when he came for his weekly visit. I waited for my mother to change her mind about leaving him and go back to him to mend their marriage—all a fairy tale.

I believe my second husband did me a great favor by leaving and not coming back. His abandonment forced me to finally face the fear of being left by someone, and opening a floodgate of grief.

A memory I did not know I had, but was told to me, returned. This was a memory of the day my mother took my sister and me away from our family home, and left my father a note. I never got to say goodbye to him, but I unconsciously grieved for him, my first love. My mother had decided that she had had enough of being married to my father, the love of my life. She packed up the house, rented a truck, and while he was at work emptied the house of its furniture, rented an apartment and moved to an undisclosed part of town. After they divorced, I waited for Sunday visits with my father; his grey Cadillac rounding the corner driving up to the front of our two-story apartment home; running down the lawn into his open arms. I grieved the loss of him. My father often said later in life: "After your mother took you I looked for you girls. No one in the family would tell me where you were."

As in all incidents in childhood, nothing was discussed, and life moved on, business as usual. My private world of imagination and make-believe continued and sustained me, a fantasy-filled world of make-believe that I carried into adulthood and into two marriages, hoping that the men I met could be transformed because of my strong will and skills at rescuing, giving and caretaking. I would do anything to make my husband well. Along with magical thinking and rescuing I took my mother's words to heart, "Do not air your dirty linen in public." "What dirty linen?" I often thought as I watched her hang the sheets on the line. But I knew it meant keeping secrets, thoughts and feelings inside me, not to be spoken aloud, not to be shared with others.

From a young age my mother's shame of me was apparent. At night, after she tucked me into bed and I fell asleep, I wet my bed. In the morning she stripped the bed, bringing the sheets down to the laundry room and sometimes rubbing my nose into the yellow circular stain, driving the shame deeper. During the nose rubbing I imagined that my knight in shining armor, my father, or a man like him would take me away and we would live happily ever after. In those moments I made a secret pledge to raise my children with unconditional love, the same love I felt from my father.

Chapter 22

Daddy arrives at eleven o'clock Sunday morning for our weekly visit. He opens the door of his silver Cadillac, steps onto the curb and lights an Old Gold cigarette. "He's here!" I shout to my mother and sister as I push open the screen door and run down the lawn into Daddy's open arms. "Look at my big girl! I love you!" Daddy says. "Look how tall you've grown in just one week's time. You are a prettier version of me. You look just like me!"

In my child's mind, my father and I were one and the same, and although I didn't grow up with him I adored him and waited each week for our Sunday visits. The other six days of the week I thought about his encouraging words: "Raven, you can do anything you put your mind to, anything at all. I believe in you. You are smart. You are beautiful and you are my daughter. You can do anything."

Thinking about his words and his love for me helped me through my day. Dreamily looking out the classroom window thinking about Daddy and our next Sunday visit helped me sit still in school and get through the day. He loved me, and that was all that mattered. Daddy would be disappointed if I did not do well in school, and I did not want to disappoint my father. Each week and before I could drive over to his house in the car he later bought for me when I was sixteen, I waited for the following Sunday, the next visiting day with Daddy so I could see him, feel his love, and hear his encouraging words. "You look like me, walk like me, think like me and act like me," and I heard, "I love you," and was elated by the warmth his message conveyed. "You look like me, walk like me, think like me and act like me," gave me an identity and the will to survive and to ignore the constant tension in the house I was growing up in without my father.

His love gave me the strength to ignore the anger, resentment and intense dislike my stepfather had for

A BLEARY-EYED STRANGER

me, resisting his daily efforts to "line me up." My stepfather bullied and ruled the house with an iron fist. At age nineteen, my sister reached her breaking point and ended up in the "Institute," as it was known in Philadelphia, the same psychiatric ward my daughter stayed in for thirty days, now renamed Kirkbride. At the Institute, my sister believed she was Queen Elizabeth. She, too, had a psychotic break from reality, hers from mental illness, while Jess's was a drug-induced psychosis. At Kirkbride, my daughter was diagnosed with a drug-induced delirium that exhibited similar schizophrenic-like symptoms as my sister's break from reality. It was my father's deep devotion to me that protected me from mental illness and drugs. I would be strong just for him. My father's love and words gave me the stability I needed to go on.

You look like me, walk like me, think like me and act like me. You can do anything. I clung to his soothing words through the long week and lonely days of childhood until Sunday when I would see him again. His words sealed my bond to him and strengthened our connection. My father's words and his unconditional love and support helped me move forward in life with confidence, faith and trust, allowing me to grow into adulthood and to finish school. My father believed in me. I would not disappoint him. I would never use drugs, drop out of school or associate with the wrong people in fear of hurting him. Although my mother left my father when I was two years old and I only saw him on Sundays for a few hours each week, I thought about him during the week and waited for his car, the silver Cadillac with matching gray leather seats, to round the corner so I could jump into his open arms.

"What would Daddy want me to do?" I often asked myself before making a decision. "How would Daddy want me to behave?" If something went wrong, I imagined my father standing by my side shaking his finger at my mother and stepfather, telling them that there were better ways to raise a child than by yelling, and I pictured my father standing next to me holding my hand. He was there for me. His love increased my ability to hold a job, earn a master's degree and become a psychotherapist and eventually study for a PhD program in Holistic Health Sciences. During the week when I wasn't with my father, I fantasized a beautiful world filled with fairies and gnomes, invisible beings that entertained, loved and supported me when my father was not around. I was independent and content with my make-believe friends, knowing I would see my father on Sundays for our weekly visit and bask in his unconditional love. His love was the only thing that mattered to me. Identifying with a strong and kind man helped me develop a sense of self. If I looked like my father, walked and talked like him like he said, perhaps I could be just like him, the kindest and gentlest person I knew. I wanted to be like him, kind and giving. My father did not drink alcohol except on holidays when a glass of wine was part of the Jewish religious ceremony at Passover.

The identification with him that formed my childhood mind helped me grow, and I believed the same identification would take root in my daughter and help her on her journey through life. My daughter would identify with me like I did with my father. She would never drink or use drugs as her father, aunts and uncles did, or inherit addiction traits because she was not exposed to it—besides she was just like me, as I was like my father. My daughter would pursue spirituality with the same fervor as I had. She would embrace the spiritual life. At the time, I did not know that addiction, which has a strong genetic component in families, can sometimes outweigh the socialization aspect of development. I denied any serious risk of addiction in my daughter because she was just like me, the way I was like my father. She was raised in a home with meditation and spirituality with knowledge of dreams, and striving for an Ascended Master Consciousness, a God-like state of unconditional love. She would embrace life and protect her body, mind and soul and not pollute it with alcohol or drugs.

Chapter 23

Jess's Childhood

"It's time for bed," I say to my baby girl, placing her on her belly and turning out the overhead light. The night light next to the crib comforts her. Gently I rub her back and tiptoe out of the room. From the doorway I watch as she rolls over and grips the bars of the crib. Pulling herself up, her head thrown back, mouth wide open, she utters a high-pitched shriek, a wail of frustration and anger, and silent words, "Why don't you pick me up?" Tiny fingers shake the rails.

My daughter is determined to tumble out of the crib and fall onto the carpet. Hopping from one foot to the other, stretching on tippy toes, Jess puts her small bow-shaped legs on the top of the crib, gaining enough momentum to topple over and out of the crib onto the floor. She runs into the living room, gleefully jumping into my open arms. Breathing in shaky breaths, tears streaming down soft cheeks, silky black lashes sparkle with salty tears. I pick Jess up kissing puffy pink baby cheeks, wiping a wet tear-stained face; droopy red eyes squeezed tightly shut. She wails, her mouth shaped in a round indignant wide-open "O."

"She can outcry me," I told my father when my daughter was eighteen months old. "She shakes the bars of the crib and wails, waiting for me to come into her room and pick her up. She calms down when I take her out of her crib and walk her around the apartment or push her in the carriage down the street or a drive around town."

"Do you want to go for a ride?" I say to her. When I can no longer bear her crying, Jess and I go for a drive. Long rides in the car seat until she falls asleep. Lifting her out of the car, patting her back, I carry my sweet sleeping girl back to her room and gently lower her into her crib.

"It hurts me to let her cry like that," I tell my

father, twisting the landline cord around my hand and dragging it down the hall, peeking around the corner into my daughter's room, quietly watching my furious, red-faced baby cry. "She can't be consoled. I feel like I'm doing everything wrong," I sigh, tired of the ongoing nighttime battles, the bedtime struggles that continue as I raise my only child without help from Jim, who is struggling with his addiction.

"Go outside and stand on the balcony so you won't hear her cry," says my father.

"I can hear her through the patio door." Cupping the receiver, pulling the pink cardigan sweater tightly around my shoulders. I step onto the balcony. Jess is eighteen months old, and I follow my father's words of wisdom, standing in the cold, shivering out on the balcony of our home, a condo in downtown Philadelphia, listening to Jess cry. Sliding the glass door open, I walk into the living room and down the hall to Jess's bedroom, decorated with soft smiling teddy bears and giraffes. A zoo of baby animals and yellow daffodil wallpaper borders the walls. A child's room with children's books spills off the bookcase, *Busy Day Busy People, Dr. Seuss, and Winnie the Pooh* are scattered across the floor next to plastic buckets filled with red, blue, green and yellow oversized Lego blocks stacked one on top of the other; a night-light merry-go-round with ceramic horses moves up and down singing a soothing lullaby. Buster, a fat gray furry stuffy toy with stubby legs and a large protruding belly, lies face down on the floor. Picking Buster up and hugging him, a favorite stuffed animal, I comb his matted fur with my fingers and wave his bear paw in the air, making the stuffed animal dance, hoping my daughter will laugh, sleepy eyes sealed shut, pink cheeks swollen and puffed round like a blowfish, wiping her tears. I pick up my girl and carry her and dancing Buster into the living room, kissing my daughter's cheeks, tasting the sweet, salty mixture of sadness and despair.

Chapter 24

When I was eight months pregnant and happily anticipating the birth of my daughter, a picture of my unborn child floated into a dream one night, legs slightly bowed. "Nothing to worry about," a dream voice said, but I woke up knowing something was wrong with my unborn child's legs. After Jess was born, the small bones in her calves were shaped like bows, as was told to me in the dream. For several months she slept in plaster casts and metal braces to straighten her legs.

At three years old, Jess began sharing her dreams with me. Dream sharing became a morning routine. One day when she was seven years old, she woke up excited to tell me her dream. "Mom," she said, rubbing the sleep from her eyes, "I dreamed that I won the candy corn contest at school today. Yesterday, in school, the teacher asked all of us to guess how many candy corns were in a glass jar. I guessed that there were 324 candy corns, but the voice in the dream said there were 328 candy corns. Should I change my answer?"

"What candy corn contest?" I inquired, distracted by the morning's chores. Checklist: breakfast, lunch, money for snacks, homework in book bag. Jess is ready for school. "Hurry and get dressed or you'll be late." Head bent, I pull the white striped polo shirt over her head.

"But last night, a voice in my dream told me that I won the candy-corn contest! The correct answer was 328 candy corns. Maybe I should change my answer so I can win?"

"Well," I said, giving her a piece of toast in one hand and a glass of chocolate milk in the other, "If the dream voice said you won the candy corn contest, I would stick with the answer you wrote down yesterday and taped to the bottom of the candy corn jar at school."

That afternoon, a happy, sweet, smiling child hopped off the bus waving a bag of yellow, white and orange candy corns. "I won! I won!" she shouted, shaking the plastic bag filled with the conical striped candy. "The dream was right, and I won! The right answer was 328 candy corns," Jess said breathlessly. I was the closest to the right number and I won! I didn't change my answer and I won!" So began our spiritual journey together, weaving its way at night through dreams. The birth of my daughter was a gift to our family, a precious gift to me.

Chapter 25

When my daughter was thirteen years old, a few months after her Bat Mitzvah and after her stepfather left the note that said he needed time alone, I smelled something burning in Jess's room. "What's that awful smell?" I said, watching Jess burn the plastic soda bottle with the neck burned off. A few months later I awoke to a knock on the front door from the police.

"Who's there?" I asked, wondering who it could be at three o'clock in the morning. A man in a blue uniform with a shiny silver badge identified himself as a police officer from the 89th Philadelphia Precinct. He handed me a piece of paper.

"Ma'am, your daughter is at the police station.

She stole your car, went on a joy ride, about a mile from here. We almost drew our guns," the policeman said, shaking his head. "Lucky for her we didn't shoot. When your daughter and her friend jumped out of the car and ran into the bushes we saw we were dealing with a bunch of small kids. They could have been shot, ma'am. Your daughter took your car and crashed it into the side of another car, but that owner isn't going to press charges. It was lucky that no one got hurt." I rushed into Jess's room to see if she was gone – she was – and raced back to the front door. The policeman asked, "Why did she do that?" Shaking his head, he handed me a ticket and walked away in disbelief.

I didn't have answers, except one. I now knew where the dent on the rear bumper of my car came from. It had not happened at the mall as my daughter had said when I noticed the dent.

"Someone backed into your car at the mall," Jess had said, covering up the fact that she had stolen the car and taken it on a joy ride. That night, a few weeks before the police officer came to my home, I slept blissfully unaware that my daughter had stolen the family car before. This joy ride was not her first.

"You have to go live with your father," I told Jess

on the ride home from the police station. "You are out of control and I cannot handle it anymore."

A few weeks later, she had had enough of living with her father and his new family. She walked three miles through the park back to our home in winter without a jacket and snow on the ground.

"I can't live with them anymore! They're not my family!" she shouted as she walked in the door.

It would be many years later that I would be forced to come out of denial and face the fact that my daughter demonstrated many high-risk behaviors throughout adolescence, pointing to an addictive personality. In Al-Anon, a program of recovery for families and friends coping with the disease of a loved one's addiction, I began to face my denial. As a psychotherapist it is easier to see another person's denial. A client's denial can be examined objectively. But Jess is my daughter; I could not acknowledge her destructive high-risk behaviors. I could not see her depression. In my mind my daughter was perfect. She would never do anything to hurt me. She was a spiritual person who viewed the body as a temple, as I did. The body was to be taken care of, never hurt or defiled by doing drugs or drinking alcohol.

Before my daughter became an addict, I believed that my love for her was all that was needed for her to grow into a healthy adult, someone who would never use drugs or drink alcohol. Throughout Jess's life I took care of and protected her, drove her to school and after school sports and activities, signed her up for summer camp, making sure she had new clothes and the sneakers she wanted, as well as inviting friends to our house on the weekends or after school. There were many play dates and fun times in our home. Children came after school and stayed for dinner. My daughter had several best friends. During her childhood we had sleepovers. Our house was a fun, relaxed place for Jess and her friends. As a parent who tried to make a good life for their child, my grief and guilt continued on through my daughter's active addiction until I came to Al-Anon and embraced the psychological changes I needed to make, letting go of guilt and self-blame.

Chapter 26

Swept along by the demands of running a household and raising a three-year-old child, I forgot about a spiritual mission leaving for the Philippines to study with the Psychic Surgeons, healers that open the body with the hands. One night, I had a dream in which I was traveling with a group of people talking about the psychic surgeons who live in the Philippines. In the morning I remembered the missionary who said she and her husband were organizing a trip to the Philippines. I went searching for a calendar. Didn't she say her group was leaving for the Philippines on October 22? In the dream it said I would be traveling soon, on October 22.

A BLEARY-EYED STRANGER

A few days later I phoned the missionary. "Is there still room on the trip? I have a three-year-old daughter Jess that would have to come with me," I told her over the phone. "Can I bring her?" I was hoping she would not turn me down. "Not a problem," she replied. "She'll love to be in the healing energy of the psychic surgeons and the group."

"Have fun and be brave," my husband Jim reassured me as he always did. He did not know I was going in search of answers about our marriage.

A few weeks later, as the cab drove away, I wondered how I would ever manage without Jim. I questioned my decision to travel to an unknown country with a group of strangers with a three-year-old without support from her father. But I could not leave my daughter behind. Where I went, my daughter went. Now, on the airplane, gently rocking the sleeping child on my lap, I regretted my decision. The Philippines were over twenty hours away, halfway around the world!

Coping with jet lag, we arrived at the hotel in the Philippines and went to sleep. At 5am we were greeted with wake-up calls from roosters and hens crowing in the yard outside the window of our hotel room. Lying in the pre-dawn hotel room with nothing to do, adjusting to the laid-back energy of "Equator Time," the slang expression the missionary, our tour guide used to mollify our speedy Western temperament, coping with jet lag, we waited to meet with the psychic surgeons. But the psychic surgeons and healers would not be available to see us for another week!

Several phone calls to Jess's father eased the dull ache in my heart. He reassured me that my adventure was something I needed to do. After a week of doing nothing, I wanted to go home. But then the tour guide announced that our time had come to see "the Sister," as one of the psychic surgeons was known.

Our small tour group that had ventured halfway around the world was ushered into a chapel filled with chickens, roosters, dogs, and cats. Children ran through open-air doorways. Weary but excited at the prospect of meeting the psychic surgeons, we filed silently into the chapel and onto the pulpit. Sister Josephina stood in the center of the group. My daughter walked onto the pulpit and fell asleep at her feet. Sister Josephina spoke directly to me.

"You are thinking of leaving the trip," she said, startling me with her statement of fact. How did she know? Only one other group member knew the difficulty I had adjusting to this new place halfway around the world with a three-year-old who missed her father and asked for him. Only one person knew about my plans to leave the trip.

"If you do leave," Sister Josephina added gloomily, beads of sweat bubbling above her lip and on her forehead, "you will have regrets." Tears welled up in my eyes and splashed down my cheeks.

Instantly the perky tour guide was by my side. Taking my hand, she whispered comfortingly, "She means you'll feel bad if you suddenly leave the group and go home without completing the three weeks." She wiped my eyes with her handkerchief. Sister Josephina was right, but I was homesick. The time away from home in the hot sun and stark hotel room with a three-year-old asking, "Where's Daddy?" had taken a toll. I wanted to go home.

That evening, as I stood in front of the hotel overlooking the beautiful, silent waters of the South Pacific, a man walked by and introduced himself. "I am one of the psychic surgeons scheduled to meet with your group tomorrow," he said. Soft brown eyes searched my face.

"I want to know about the future of my marriage

with my husband and his addiction," I blurted out. "I don't want to get divorced." As a child I made a silent vow that I would never divorce. I would not put my child through what I had been through. "What can I do to prevent it?" I was hoping he could give me an easy remedy that would take away the pain of divorce. I was afraid I would not have another opportunity to ask my question, the reason I had traveled halfway around the world.

The dark-haired man took my hand and replied, "Soon you'll be separating from your husband." The ashen look on my face told him the impact of his words. This could not be true! I would save our marriage and stop my husband's drinking and drug use. I was strong enough and had the power to do it.

The psychic healer patted my shoulder and added, "Put positive affirmations under your pillow. Perhaps that will help your marriage." But he had spoken the truth, and soon after that meeting my daughter and I left for home.

My daughter does not remember that trip to the Philippines when she was three years old. She does remember the day her father left on his motorcycle for his cross-country trip touring cities and countryside across the United States, leaving us behind. She remembers the note and the feeling of abandonment when her stepfather left, saying, "I need time alone."

Chapter 27

Why did my Jess become an addict? She first began using drugs and drinking alcohol in ninth grade when she was fourteen years old, and later her addiction landed her on the streets in Kensington in Philadelphia. Still believing I had influenced her in some way, I asked myself these tormenting questions over and over again:

Perhaps my daughter began using drugs because the men in her life, her father and stepfather, left her at a young age.

Perhaps she began using drugs because of the time I went to the headmaster's office at the elite private school she attended demanding that her third-grade teacher stop writing Jess's name on the blackboard even though my daughter had shouted out of turn in class and was clearly in the wrong.

"It scares me when the teacher writes my name on the blackboard," she said when she came home after school. The next day I went to school to right the wrong. "Do not write her name on the board, it scares her," I told the headmaster. In my eyes my daughter was never wrong.

Or the time the school offered her after-school help, saying she had a reading problem. Not my daughter. Any problems Jess had I would handle.

Perhaps it was the time when she was ten years old and fumbled the ball on the soccer field running in the wrong direction down the field as the coach and players shouted at her, "You're running the wrong way!"

"What the heck is she doing?" the mayor, whose daughter also went to that same elite private school, asked as he proudly watched his sour-faced daughter kick the ball and run down the field to score a goal, while my daughter's head hung in shame.

Perhaps Jess remembers at two years old my sobbing in front of a safe emptied of cash from the family business, all of the money gone, spent on drugs.

Or perhaps it was my daughter's announcement

mid-year tenth grade that she would not return to the elite private school that was supposed to guarantee she would never turn to drugs; filling in the missing parts with tutors, after school sports and activities. But in tenth grade Jess wanted out. "I am leaving school and I want to go to a public school where people don't make fun of the purple and green streaks in my hair."

Or was it the time my daughter refused to go to camp and got off the bus on Broad Street and I carried her home her legs flailing behind her kicking and screaming, "I don't want to go to camp! I don't like the kids and the sports and I'm not good at anything."

Perhaps it was my decision not to get her vaccinated until she was five years old.

Or the day I told the dentist not to x-ray her skull. "I don't need a panoramic view of her teeth," I said as we were asked to leave the dentist's office and never return.

But more likely it was the time I brought her homework left on the dining room table up to school.

"Never do that again!" My daughter shrieked, her face red. Embarrassing her was the last thing I intended when I handed her homework to her fourth-grade teacher hoping she wouldn't be penalized.

(Her classmates staring at the mother who arrived breathlessly mid-morning waving the forgotten homework brought to school for her ten-year-old girl).

Or maybe it was the time I dropped her off at a kindergarten interview at a private school, part of their process to assess if she would fit in. Waiting outside the classroom peeking in, my daughter stood there not knowing what to do. Five minutes, ten minutes—long enough! I rushed back in, grabbed her hand and left that school behind.

"I was just coming to get her," the teacher ran after me, but I was gone and I was right. My daughter should not have had to wait so long.

Always protecting my daughter.

Maybe it was the time that a stranger at the condo where we lived in downtown Philadelphia shouted, "Stop carving your name on the table with that pencil!" She reached for her hand. "I'll handle it," I said, pushing her hand away from my daughter. "But you're not handling it!" she shrieked as I took my daughter's hand and walked away, ignoring the pencil marks on the lacquered wood table in the lobby carved by my daughter.

Or perhaps it was the time her Montessori teacher

raced after us shaking her finger, "You took the eraser without asking!" My four-year-old looked up trustingly, lovingly and wrapped her tiny hand around mine. "No worries it's okay," I whispered. "I'm sure she didn't mean to take it," I said, looking at my daughter and back at the teacher, wondering why she was making such a big deal, secretly worried that perhaps there was some reason I should be concerned; something I didn't know, didn't want to know, something wrong with my daughter—quickly dismissing the thought. Nothing could be wrong with Jess. And if there were a problem, I would take care of it.

"I will handle it," I said.

"It was an accident," I said to the teacher as we walked down the street away from the Montessori school, pushing the incident into the back of my mind, thinking about her father lying drunk on the couch, the money locked in the safe now gone—and no way to keep the nightclub, a family business Jim and I owned in downtown Philadelphia, open and pay our bills.

Perhaps it was the time my daughter repeatedly protested that she was not the one who had ripped a hole in my Day Timers appointment book.

"I didn't do it. I didn't do it!" She cried over and

over again. "Do you believe me? Please believe me."

"Of course I believe you, my daughter." My precious sweet child who is just like me; my daughter would never lie or take anything that did not belong to her; secretly wondering about her need to convince me of her innocence, so adamant, pushing away the nagging feeling into the back of my mind, "What is wrong with Jess?" Nothing could be wrong with my little girl who is just like me.

Or perhaps it was the first day at Montessori school, Jess pushing her way to the front of the line wanting to be first, always wanting to be first. But the other children shouted. "Go to the back of the line!" they chanted in unison, but I was slow to pull her back, always afraid to hurt her feelings, afraid she could not handle life, a child who was slow to come into this world.

Deep down, I believed it happened at birth.

"You are eight centimeters dilated," the doctor said. "It's time to give you Pitocin." This is a hormone that causes the uterus to contract and bring on labor. The doctor administered the artificial stimulation, rushing my baby girl into the world, a place she was slow to embrace.

Perhaps it was the fact that she would stand in her crib at night and outcry me. "I don't know what to do!" I told my father when my daughter was eighteen months old, wailing, gripping and shaking the bars of the crib.

"When I put her in her crib she cries for hours," I told my father. "Go stand out on the balcony so you don't hear her cry." My father's advice did not help. I could always hear my daughter crying, always feel her need to be held, the attention she needed, the pain in her heart.

Or maybe it was the time I took her halfway around the world to the Philippines to see the psychic surgeons looking for answers to my failing marriage from her father, searching for a prediction about the future. I was determined to make my marriage work. I would make it work, could make it work. My husband would stop drinking and using drugs. I would never get divorced. But in reality, I was tired of hiding the addiction. I wasn't raised with alcohol in my family and I didn't want my daughter to see it at home.

Possibly it was during adolescence. "I'm not going back to that private school," she said, throwing her book bag onto the backseat of the car, the school that my father paid twelve thousand dollars a year for my daughter to attend. Jess's arms folded across her chest. Her purple-green dyed bangs fell over her eyes.

Perhaps it was her determination to buy a guitar. "I want that guitar!" my nine-year-old child is pointing to an eight-hundred-dollar red lacquered electric Gibson guitar, a present she wants for her birthday. "Can I have it?"

"Let me think about it," I say, secretly thrilled that my pre-teen wants to play an instrument, hoping she will latch on to something that she loves that will make her happy; a hobby to keep her focused and on the right path, a life filled with success and happiness, and on the way to rock star fame. I buy the eight-hundred-dollar Gibson guitar for her next birthday.

Perhaps it was the bad advice from a psychiatrist who said, "Put a lock on your bedroom door. Make Jess sleep in her own room or on the floor outside of your locked door."

Perhaps it was at the swimming pool at the condo in Philadelphia where we lived when she jumped off the diving board, the older girls teasing her because she was so small. Bouncing a toy rubber knife on my hand, letting the older girls know I was a force to be reckoned with, I glared at them. I would protect Jess, take care of her and make sure that no harm would come to her. No one would laugh or tease Jess.

My daughter would never experience loneliness or depression as I had in my childhood, coping with chronic bed wetting and damp sheets. During eight weeks of summer camp I was nicknamed "faucet" for crying and waiting for summer to end when I was eight years old. My daughter would never have these experiences of rejection, abandonment, loneliness or isolation. She would count and not be invisible as I was. She would have friends. She was nurtured, affirmed and unconditionally loved. She would be smart, go to the best schools and colleges, never lose her place in class when reading aloud or forget where her book bag was, or not be able to make friends. She would never have a stepfather who poked her in the chest shouting, "You idiot! Go to your room."

My daughter does remember, however, the man who would someday become her stepfather, a man who lived with us for eight years and was like a father to her. The man who said, "I need time alone" and left a note which ended the marriage, disappearing one night from our lives forever, while I searched for healing from a broken heart, finally going to Co-dependents Anonymous meetings to look for answers for my failed marriage. Through the grief and loss process, I continued to provide a stable home for my daughter, protecting her from the loss of her stepfather and her father's addiction, reminding myself that Jess was more like me and that addiction did not run in my family genes. Jess was strong and resilient. She would recover from her grief and losses, and if she didn't see substances in the home she would never turn to drugs or alcohol or get caught in the nightmare of addiction.

Still trying to make Jess's life right and blaming myself, I asked her, "What *did* I do wrong?" Looking for the reason she turned to drugs, always looking for reasons when *addiction is a disease that runs in families* was not a good enough answer. At those times, I was still blaming myself for not being the perfect mother. Why else would she turn to heroin? I asked the unanswerable question, driving the shame and guilt deeper.

"What is the one thing that you can pinpoint that I did wrong?" I asked her as if there were one simple answer, sure I had failed her. I wanted to know what made her pick up and use drugs.

If I did something wrong, what could I do to make it better so she would stop using drugs before she was arrested or died? I was trying to control what I can never control. If only I found the one thing where I went wrong I would change it and she would be cured. Life would move forward and I would be free from the struggle and worry.

I wanted my daughter to say that I had done nothing wrong and that her addiction came from her father's side of the family. Wasn't her father's family filled with people who struggled with alcohol and drug addiction? When my daughter was in her early thirties and her struggle with alcohol and drugs became known to the family. When I was sixty-six years old and began my program of recovery in Al-Anon for families and friends who suffer the fall-out from the disease of addiction, I was sure that I had contributed to the disease that made her an addict.

Chapter 28

Still I continued to question my parenting skills.

What if I hadn't let Jess sit in front of the television to eat dinner and do homework as she once suggested was the one thing I did wrong?

What if I could say no and not feel guilty, and set clear, consistent boundaries?

What if I had let Jess cope with the consequences of forgetting her homework?

What if I hadn't filled out the college applications for her in 12th grade?

What If I had accepted the social worker's invitation at Fairmount Hospital to attend Al-Anon meetings when Jess was three years old and her father went into his recovery program?

What if I didn't believe that you had to keep giving and giving without any thought of where the money was going or if it would ever be paid back?

What if I stopped people-pleasing and put the focus on myself, as Al-Anon suggested?

What if I had played sports with her and taught her the rules of the game?

What if when she was fifteen years old I had forbidden her to go downtown and hang on South Street with no supervision, hoping a fifteen-year-old would make the right decisions?

What if I hadn't let her drive until she was eighteen years old? She could have avoided car accidents that put her life at risk, or perhaps not become addicted to drugs. *"More than 64,000 Americans died from a drug overdose in 2016, including illicit drugs and prescription opioids – nearly double in a decade."* [8] "Why is this happening?" I ask, still grieving the loss of what life was supposed to look like, with a child who could hold a job and take care of her bills.

While my daughter was managing chronic pain

---

8. https://drugpolicy.org/issues/drug-overdose

she got addicted to painkillers, which eventually progressed to opioids. Growing up, Jess demonstrated high risk behavior which increased during adolescence, full-blown in her thirties. Her addiction crept up on her and neither her father nor I saw the signs.

Chapter 29

"You threw out all of the furniture!" my daughter is home for a visit.

I threw everything out, the way I dealt with all of the losses from the addiction. It doesn't make rational sense—I felt out of control. When I started going to Al-Anon I felt helpless. I didn't know what to do, so I threw out furniture, the dining room table, the black leather couch and other things. Hopeless and afraid, I called 1-800 Haul-Out, pointing to sofas, lawn chairs and glass tables.

"It was a way to get rid of old memories," I told Jess. "At the time, I didn't want to live here anymore but I couldn't run away so I threw everything out.

Looking back, throwing out furniture didn't make any difference. I am still powerless over your addiction and I just want you to recover. Throwing out the old furniture didn't give me the fresh start I anticipated. It left me with an empty house, my heart broken and afraid. Al-Anon meetings saved my life. My perspective changed. I began to see you as someone struggling to conquer an addiction, not someone who relapses over and over again, a moral failing, a weakness of character, but a person trying to live a sober life. Attending Al-Anon was life changing."

Six years later I was asked to be the Spiritual Speaker at the State Al-Anon Convention, sharing my experience, strength and hope. Here's what I said.

My Al-Anon Story

I didn't grow up in an alcoholic family, but I grew with what Al-Anon calls the ISMS: Arrogance-ism Grandiosity-ism Distancing-ism Anger-ism Isolation-ism. I later married an alcoholic, someone I could rescue, take care of and make whole. I didn't think I had a problem. I was whole. I had degrees. I didn't come from an alcoholic home. At the time I married,

I didn't know my then-husband was an alcoholic. But I needed him and his family, he needed me, we were young, and my love was strong enough for the both of us. But what brought me into Al-Anon was my hope that my commitment to meetings would help my daughter. I was glad to be there as I was grieving the grief and pain of her addiction, but I had a lot to learn. I didn't know that at the time; I only knew that I was in a safe place, where people listened when I shared. They did not comment, but they looked concerned, like they cared. That was good enough for me. And in meetings, I cried and cried for the first three to four years, and the people in my meetings listened. I was in the right place, the only place for me to be.

When I came into Al-Anon, I felt that I had a special relationship with my Higher Power. I taught meditation and I was on a spiritual mission to raise people's consciousness through meditation. But this spiritual grandiosity, as I call it, soon came into perspective. There were many people in the Al-Anon meetings of all ages who were also developing a special relationship with their higher power but did not feel the need— or so I thought—to help others grow in their spiritual consciousness. They were placing the emphasis on themselves. I, on the other hand, was other-focused.

I didn't grow up in an alcoholic family, but my first marriage was to a man who was an alcoholic—something I suspected when we were walking down the aisle and I smelled alcohol. I stopped walking, but my father gave me a gentle little push, and so it begins.

When I was two years old, my mother was twenty-four and decided she had had enough of being married to my father, the love of my life. She packed up the house one day, rented a truck and while he was at work, she took my sister, who was four, and me, cleared out the household furniture, rented an apartment and moved to an undisclosed part of town. Although I was only two years old, I grieved the loss of him. "I looked for you girls. No one in the family would tell me where you were," my father often said later in life.

When I was five years old my mother, sister and I moved to a second-floor walk-up apartment in a neighborhood of homes. When you came through the front door to the apartment there was a trapdoor, a hole in the floor that led to the basement and the washing machines. When Mom was in the basement doing laundry, the 5 by 10 trapdoor was propped up on a hinge and leaned against the wall. Mom would yell, "Trap door is open!" My sister and I raced in from outside and had one second to stop at the front door and get our footing, to keep from falling through the hole in the floor. Then we would inch our backs against the wall, balancing ourselves on the remaining five-inch floorboard and run upstairs to our apartment. One day, my best friend came into the apartment and fell through the trap door hole, and I watched as she tumbled down a flight of steps, landing with a thud on the cement basement floor. Mom quickly gathered her up, propped her up on a stool, and covered her with mercurochrome head to toe, as I stared in terrified amazement thinking, "Is she injured? What would have happened if she had died? And what can mercurochrome possibly do in this situation?" My friend was covered from head to toe in orange medicine.

As in all incidents in childhood, nothing was discussed, life moved on, business as usual, and I lived in my own private world of imagination and make-believe. A rich world of make believe that I carried into adulthood and into three marriages, hoping I could transform the men I met with my excellent skills at rescuing, giving, and caretaking. And I would do anything to make the men well. Along with magical thinking and rescuing I always remembered Mom's words, "Do not air your dirty linen in public." "What dirty linen?" I thought, watching her hang the sheets on the line. But I knew it meant keeping secrets, thoughts and feelings to myself. From a young age, I felt my mother's shame of me. A deep sleeper, at night, after she tucked me into bed, I wet my bed. Night after night, day in and day out, she was exasperated; taking the sheets off the bed, bringing them down to the laundry room, and sometimes, in her frustration, she rubbed my nose into the sheets, driving the shame deeper increasing the fantasy that my knight in shining armor—my father, or a man like my father—would take me away and we would live happily ever after.

When I was seven years old, my Cinderella fantasy hit the wall of reality. My mother re-married my stepfather, a man determined to change me. In his world, filled with rage, he wanted me to "line up" and to obey him. His anger and sexual innuendos towards my sister and me drove the shame deeper. But my fantasy life was a private and joyful place. I imagined beings of light, fairies and gnomes around me that lived in the honeysuckle bush and came from the sky, protecting me. I loved being outdoors; nature was my refuge. At night before bed, I blessed all of the people I knew and much to the chagrin of my stepfather, wrote their names in pencil on the wall beside my bed blessing each one of them, neighbors, friends, pets, the milkman. Even as a young child I felt and believed in a spiritual presence, something protecting and guiding me.

I saw my knight in shining armor—my father—on Sundays, and I pined for him the other days of the week. He was my rock and someone I did not want to disappoint, and the reason I could sit still in class and do my work even though I had no idea what was going on all the way to 12th grade. While I sat in school I thought about my father knowing he would be coming on Sunday and the thought of him, his unconditional warmth and love, comforted me. My father gave me an identity. He often said, "You look like me. You talk like me. You think like me. You act like me." The contrast of my father and his love for me, and my tyrannical abusive stepfather exercising his will and his authority over me, created two distinct realities. In one reality, I was always trying to escape, and I did run away from home when I was a teenager hitchhiking, getting into strange men's cars, sleeping in cold beds in homes of people I did not know. The second reality was waiting for my knight in shining armor, my father, to come and rescue me. This running away and keeping secrets meant that when I reached adolescence I was shut down and withdrawn, I couldn't make friends, and when people liked me I didn't know why. Looking back, I was depressed, anxious and wanting to escape. This split from my feelings and the running away in my mind literarily kept me away from the pain of what was going on at home. Living with rage-oholics, distancers where I was always wrong, I felt oppressed, lonely and sad. And I pushed the pain and shame deep and far away from me the joy of my fantasies protecting and sustaining me. The unspoken message in the home was be quiet, dress up, look good and above all else, do not under any circumstances embarrass me. But I was an embarrassment and shame to my mother and to my stepfather, and I felt it and I carried it in my heart.

I didn't grow up with the disease of alcoholism, but I grew up with other isms; abandonment, coldness, estrangement and secrets, hiding the shame and later when my mother remarried, I experienced anger and control that was abusive. I was shut down and found comfort with my sister. At night, I would sneak into her room and wrap my arms around her. Like my father, she was my comfort. When I was thirteen years old I started running away from home, staying out, hitchhiking, afraid of the present, afraid of the future. One time I called my father, not wanting him to worry, and asked if I could come live with him. He told me I had to go home and live with my mother—a sobering splash of cold water. Where was my knight, my rescuer? But I forgave him everything, always forgave him. So I went home to: don't talk, don't share, don't tell anyone what is going on in our house; the rage, the excessive punishment, while mother worked and my stepfather was in charge.

When I was seventeen years old, after much struggle through school, I was accepted into my first college CW Post on Long Island New York, on probation. After freshman year I was asked to leave. I kept missing classes, making up my own reality, ignoring the rules. My second college, Villanova University, was night school, and there I began to grow up and follow rules as best I could, always rebellious. I eventually transferred to Oglethorpe University, Atlanta Georgia, where I graduated and later went on to graduate school at Tulane University.

During graduate school a new spiritual life unfolded. In graduate school I moved into spiritual ashrams, waking at dawn meditating and praying, teaching meditation classes in the evening and spending countless hours on spiritual retreats. I had a deep desire to know my relationship with my higher power. When I was twenty-seven I moved to Israel. There my mother came for a short visit. She said she had seen my childhood sweetheart, Jim, giving her stamp of approval for my first marriage. So I came home and down the aisle I went, alcohol on his breath. Who cared? I could transform him. Make him perfect in every way.

"He seems like a good guy," she had said to me when she was visiting Israel about the man who was going to be my first husband, but he suffered from the disease of alcoholism. And true to form, through the marriage to my first husband, I hid the pain and the secret of the disease that was destroying our family, throwing out the bottles and paraphernalia and hiding everything from my family. To this day they do not know that my first husband is an alcoholic and to this day they don't know that he has been sober for forty years. Throughout the marriage his addiction increased, we lost our nightclub business, our money, and our relationship and eventually we divorced, and all of that hiding made me sick. A few years before I had my daughter, desperately wanting a child, making up for the child Jim and I lost before we were married, I ended up in the hospital with gastrointestinal issues on a hyperalimentation machine which force-fed me through the chest for three weeks. I had been sick for a year but didn't tell anyone, keeping it secret, and everything got progressively worse and out of control. The medical staff talked about giving me a colostomy. I was thirty-two years old. I could not get well. Then, like an angel, a nurse sat down on my bed and said, "You have to make yourself well." Her words began the healing process for me.

A few years later we had our daughter. When she was three years old, I decided that since I hadn't grow up in an alcoholic home, and since this marriage was failing, it was best that I leave my daughter's father as I did not want her growing up with alcohol and drugs in our home. I knew nothing about the disease of alcoholism. And when my first husband went into recovery, I turned down the social worker's suggestion that I attend Al-Anon meetings. Why would I need to go? We didn't have alcohol in our home.

A BLEARY-EYED STRANGER

The divorce, I believed, would protect my daughter from the problems of future addiction. She would never be exposed to the same substance abuse problems that her father had struggled with. I believed that without him, alcohol and drugs would be out of our lives forever. I had my fantasies, my grandiosity and my arrogance. I had much to learn.

Fast-forward some thirty years later, and the news of our daughter's addiction came to me like this. My ex-husband texted and said, "She is riding up and down the turnpike high as a kite." Our daughter's addiction, something I was sure would never happen to her, came to light. I went to Al-Anon, desperate to find relief from the intense anxiety and fear I was trying to control, fear for my daughter's life. In Al-Anon I learned that alcoholism is a family disease. My daughter had perhaps inherited the disease; her father, her grandfather, as well as her aunts and uncles suffer from it too. And so, after turning down the suggestion from the social worker from the hospital where Jim went for recovery who suggested Al-Anon years before, I finally walked into my first meeting, desperate and grieving, and so very afraid.

I traveled to meetings in neighborhoods far away from home, not wanting to bump into anyone I knew, hiding my shame and feelings of failure. In the meetings I learned that I hadn't caused the disease. I couldn't cure it and I definitely could not control it. As time progressed, I also learned about the 12 "Steps" and 12 "Traditions," and later, when I became involved in service in Al-Anon, the "Concepts" guidelines for service. In the beginning and for many years, I dragged my heels, resentful that I had to be in Al-Anon meetings, and I waited to "get it" and graduate. Only recently, eight years later, at seventy-four years old, have I now given up the fantasy and understand it as a life-long self-discovery process.

When I walked into the first meeting I thought, "I have a relationship with a higher power, so why am I here? Where is Jim? Sure, he has forty years in recovery, but I'm the one sitting in meetings." But I had an ulterior motive. I was certain that if I attended meetings, I could nip my daughter's addiction in the bud. I needed to go to meetings for her, get through it and help her get her addiction under control. I could do this, protect her, make sure she stayed alive. But I soon learned I could not do that. I would have to face reality. My daughter had an addiction that I could not control.

In Al-Anon I learned that my childhood fantasies had been coping skills that made me happy and made me feel safe. One of the fantasies I carried into parenthood was that my daughter was like me. I had raised her. There was no alcohol or drugs in our home. She would be like me and imitate my way of living. Meditation would be life saving for her, as it had been for me. Her addiction would stop because it hurt me, and she would recognize that and stop it. "You look like me, talk like me, think like me, act like me": my father's words were special and defined my relationship with him and gave me an identity. I brought that thinking into the relationship with my daughter. So I went to Al-anon with fear, grief and loss. There I grieved and learned to deal with my fears, identifying with and learning to let go of the four "Ms": Mothering, Managing, Manipulating, Martyring. And the 3 "Cs": didn't Cause it, can't Control it, and can't Cure it. Sometimes I was hung up on the "didn't cause it." Did I cause it? I asked myself that time and time again.

I came into Al-Anon fairly certain that if Jess saw I was going to meetings and working on myself she would instantly do the same, but she was going from recovery house to recovery house living in the Badlands in Philadelphia—Ground Zero for opioids in the country. And everywhere she went her addiction got worse and I was learning the meaning of Step One, powerlessness, not submission, as that would have been dangerous in the house I grew up in, but letting go to a higher power that was leading me and teaching me, guiding us both. Trusting in my higher power, growing my trust and faith, often I would bargain and pray—keep her going, dear God, and I will do anything, anything.

As I worked the 12 steps of recovery my relationship with my higher power became stronger. I let go more and more, often taking back my will, because I have a strong will, only to be reminded that I had to let go again if I didn't want to live in chronic anxiety. I learned that Jess has her own higher power, and I was not it. What a concept for a mother. And to this day I still remind myself daily that I am not her higher power. She has her own higher power, guiding and restoring her to sanity and teaching her to trust. And she is not just like me, but a soul on her own journey, her own path.

In Al-Anon I got a sponsor and spoke about my

character defects to her; I was learning to trust. I saw myself as strong and capable and let go of the belief that emotions made me feel weak. In meetings I was vulnerable and I learned to trust others, listening and sharing their experience, strength and hope. Sharing my defects of character was humbling, but my meeting mates and my sponsor listened non-judgmentally and I made it through one of the hardest things for me to do—be vulnerable, especially with a woman.

By the sixth step my relationship with my higher power was stronger, and I was entirely ready to have my shortcomings removed, my grandiosity, my dissociation splitting off from reality, running away, keeping my feelings—the biggest one being shame—to myself. And I humbly asked my higher power to remove them. I made amends with my name at the top of the list. I made amends for not knowing and guessing what parenting and reality were all about. I forgave myself; forgave myself for not going to Al-Anon forty years ago when it was offered when Jim went into recovery. I was not ready. It took me many years of meditation and prayer as well as therapies and healing journeys to make it safe for me to open up in a roomful of strangers who became my friends.

Along with daily meditation and conscious contact with my higher power I began speaking aloud to something greater than myself, reminding myself that my higher power is in charge and directs and guides and leads, if I can just let go. I served in Al-Anon meetings, as Secretary, Treasurer, Group Representative, and Convention Chair; volunteering in the prison, delivering the Al-Anon message and now as a District Representative for Al-Anon. I served to keep myself focused on me, and I have learned to keep the focus on me. I have learned to say I am listening and contain the knee jerk response. I've learned that it is safe to reach out to my sponsor—a big lesson for me. I have learned that I can only be in charge of myself, my spirituality, my desires and expectations. My daughter and all of the other people in my life are in charge of themselves and I pray for their healing and well-being. And my daughter struggled with her addiction, smashing up the car and getting arrested, spending the night in jail, stay after hospital stay, then back to the streets: some of the darkest times. I meditated and prayed. And finally I came to terms with it; I accepted that I could not change her addiction, just as I could not change her father's addiction. But I could continue to work on myself, on my need to rescue, to take care of others, and not to forget the importance of setting boundaries. I could stop behaviors that were not working.

Al-Anon has helped me change in so many ways. I have grown spiritually. I have grown in empathy and compassion towards my daughter, her father, myself, our family and practice letting go, a daily renewal.

Jess now lives with me and has been sober for three years. My struggle has been getting out of my way and letting my higher power work through me. I try to think before I speak. I take the "Al-Anon Pause" and sometimes when I come into the house and I have had a long day I pray first, asking to stay balanced, to be a good listener, non-judgmental, knowing that my daughter has had her day too. This time we now have living together in sobriety, including emotional sobriety, is a gift. My attitude makes the difference. So what if the dishes are not done? Is that the first thing I say, did you do the dishes? I don't talk like that to a stranger. And I remind myself of my spiritual aims, patience, kindness, compassion, empathy—walking in her shoes.

There are so many miracles. Most recently my daughter went out and bought socks for the women in one of the recovery houses in Kensington where she had lived for several years. She is thinking about helping others, giving back for the help she received during her addiction to the people who are still struggling: a spiritual shift that I didn't ask or suggest she do. She did it gratefully, giving back for the miracle of her sobriety.

Today, I don't have to be ungrounded and spacey, filled with fantasy and wishful thinking, and call that spiritual. I don't have to make up reality or live in magical thinking to feel spiritual. Reality just is, for today in this moment. I don't have to make it bigger and grander than it is. It just is. But my heart can fill it with joy. I can practice a tool or tools of the program daily. There is a power in prayer. I have to ask for what I want and need, not feel embarrassed that I am asking for too much from a higher power and then let go, allowing myself to be led. Being unconditionally loving and compassionate, being grateful for all of my blessings. Not my will but Thy will, knowing that my higher power made me an emotional, spiritual being of light, and that I am a spiritual being on an earth-walk. I am also a human being seeking spiritual experiences, and expressing emotions is safe. I am teachable and don't have to be first in line with my hand up. I can let go and relax, I am safe. Waiting before I speak is healing to others and to myself, practicing neutrality staying in the middle and listening guards my serenity. And I do this best with daily renewal of conscious contact with my higher power, prayer and meditation. I have learned:

That I am powerless, but not helpless.

That there is something greater than myself that restored our family to sanity.

That each person has their own higher power, and I am not it.

That it is necessary to examine my personality so that I can grow. My self- righteousness and grandiosity and other personality flaws keep my higher power from flowing in.

That I am entirely ready to have them removed, and it feels good!

That it is safe to do and to share my 4th and 5th step with someone in Al-Anon. (4th Step: Made a searching and fearless inventory of ourselves. 5th Step: Admitted to God, to ourselves, and to another human being the exact nature of our wrongs.) I am entirely ready to have God remove my defects of character.

I make amends where possible, and I do so daily knowing that I have a program, and when I make a mistake I can say I am sorry, and I am.

I meditate and pray and make conscious contact with my higher power and listen to the still voice for direction and guidance.

Chapter 30

Jess lives with me now.

"I am motivated!" Her words to me one Sunday morning are like warm rays from the sun shining down on me, healing my heart.

"I am motivated," Jess repeats again, sipping a large caramel frappé with whipped cream. My daughter and I eat a McDonald's no-meat breakfast sandwich on the way home from the methadone clinic. After her month stay at Kirkbride, now stabilized, the delirium gone, Jess moved home with me. My daughter sleeps in the new recliner chair in our home. The rest of the afternoon she watches television and falls asleep for hours after the twelve to thirteen hours she already slept at night.

"I like the new methadone clinic, I'm happy I made the change from the Northeast Treatment Center (NET). At this new clinic they did blood work and decreased my dose of methadone. The doctor said that I wasn't absorbing it and the excess was floating around in my blood."

"Why didn't they check your blood levels at the NET?" After the delirium, Jess is taking her medication-assisted treatment seriously. She is in a new clinic and ready to change.

"I am motivated," she repeats. I breathe a sigh of relief and remind myself of my Al-Anon credo: "Stay out of her business." "Give her the dignity of recovery." "She has her own higher power." "She has her own Program." "Take care of yourself." "Contain the knee jerk reaction." "Mind your own business."

"I am glad," is all I say, thankful she is not drug seeking on the streets of Kensington but resting in the recliner chair back home. She is motivated.

I learn all I can about methadone, a medication-assisted treatment (MAT). Methadone, a synthetic opiate first made in Germany was used as an analgesic (a drug to reduce pain) in World War II and was later studied and used for drug treatment for heroin. The purpose was to wean patients off heroin with the hope that people could develop new behaviors, eliminating drug-seeking behaviors.

"Motivated," Jess repeats to herself, as I walk out the door to work, confident that she will be there sober when I return and the house will still be standing. Remembering the words from Al-Anon literature and Al-Anon member shares, I practice loving detachment, giving her the dignity to recover in the way she sees it. I close the door and silently repeat the serenity prayer: "God grant me the serenity to accept the things I cannot change, the courage to change the things I can, and the wisdom to know the difference."

"Motivated," Jess drifts off to sleep. I close the door behind me, containing the worry, fear and judgments, focusing on the glimmer of hope, the ray of sunshine after many long dreary rain-filled days that stretched into years. Recovery is hard, stressful. Jess sleeps a lot and is often agitated and stressed.

PAWS, Post-Acute Withdrawal, whether mild or serious, is a necessary process in early recovery from alcohol or other drug dependence. Think of the withdrawal syndrome as the brain's way of correcting the chemical imbalances suffered during active addiction. PAWS occurs most commonly and intensely among individuals with alcohol and opioid addiction, as well as in people with addiction to benzodiazepines (or "benzos," which are commonly prescribed for the treatment of anxiety and panic attacks), heroin (an opiate) or medically prescribed pain medication.[9] Jess is healing. She is resting. Time is needed. She is motivated.

"I should have done methadone treatment many years ago, but there is a stigma associated with taking methadone," Jess said. "People stereotype addicts as if we are bad people and use drugs on purpose. I started taking pain medication to manage chronic pain and continued to use recreationally. My brain was hijacked quickly. You know how badly I wanted to stop, Mom. That's what caused the delirium. Recently I shared at an AA meeting that I was on methadone and I felt judged. Some people in the AA Program say if you're taking methadone you're still using drugs, but it's a medicine and it's taking away the cravings and making me comfortable. I am hopeful I can stop the lifestyle

---

[9]. https://www.hazeldenbettyford.org/articles/post-acute-withdrawal-syndrome

of buying drugs on the streets. Methadone is saving my life. The methadone clinic is organized. They don't haphazardly give you the medication without doing blood work and random urine screens. It is controlled and monitored by professionals who care about people and want us to get well.

"In order to be eligible for methadone you have to go to IOP, Intensive Outpatient, three mornings a week for three hours as well as individual therapy. You have to commit to a treatment plan and follow-up. I wasn't committed before. Now I am. Not everyone wants to change and get committed, but I do. I am ready now. I want to change and besides, I won't get dosed if I don't do these things.

"Mom, did you know that the clinic takes random urine tests? It's always a surprise. They want to catch people who are using to see what level of care is needed for them if they are mixing street drugs with methadone. The clinic staff is trying to help them. Sometimes people pay others for what's called "clean urine" that won't show up with benzos, marijuana or other opiates in it because the person isn't taking drugs or drinking alcohol. People struggling with addiction think they're fooling the staff at the clinic, but they are just fooling themselves. My urine tests have been clean. I don't want to relapse. If something happens, I won't move forward at the clinic. I'll be at the same level of care and I want to move forward Mom, I really do. I want to stop methadone at some point too. But right now it is saving my life. I have been struggling for years. I tried everything, Suboxone, all different kinds of therapies and nothing worked; the cravings to pick up and use and get the euphoric high and also to stop the pain of withdrawal is brutal. If you've never struggled with addiction you can't really understand. Daddy gets it. He lived it. Even though he never took methadone, he understands addiction. Addiction takes you over, it descends like a black cloud and before you know it you're addicted. You can't stop using. Your body feels weak. It's very scary. I know it doesn't sound rational, but the reason people keep using is so they won't feel sick with body aches, chills and hot flashes, diarrhea; the pain of withdrawal is awful. I can't even describe it—you become violently ill. I wouldn't wish it on my worst enemy."

Jess is finally getting the help that works for her because she is ready. According to the government website SAMHSA, "methadone works by changing how the brain and nervous system respond to pain. It lessens the painful symptoms of opiate withdrawal and blocks the euphoric effects of opiate drugs such as heroin, morphine, and codeine, as well as semi-synthetic opiates such as Oxycodone and hydrocodone."[10]

"Daddy does understand," I tell our daughter. "He lived it and I witnessed the worst parts of it." I was the spouse of someone addicted to drugs and alcohol and now I am the mother of a child addicted to drugs, and like her father, she is finally healing. After Jess's daily methadone dose and when she has finished her weekly nine hours of Intensive Outpatient group therapy (IOP), she comes home and relaxes in the recliner, the one I bought so she would have space in the living room to relax, watch television, play video games, and drink her favorite drink now: vanilla Ensure.

"Ensure is delicious, Mom, and I only like the vanilla kind. Don't bring me any other kind, the vanilla is the best." After she has drunk dozens of eight-ounce bottles I ask, "An Ensure addiction?"

"Let's not get carried away," she says, laughing. She is more grounded, although nothing is funny anymore. "I lost my sense of humor," I admit.

---

10. https://www.samhsa.gov/medication-assisted-treatment/treatment/methadone

"Left it in Kensington on the street." I watch her closely. She sleeps or plays Final Fantasy, a video game.

When she was first living at home and getting "motivated," Jess gave me money she made from her job to hold for her. Later, she opened an account and began managing her own money.

Families have asked me for a formula for what to do, how to proceed. My advice to parents is to do what works for you. Jess is in sobriety on methadone and healing. This is working for her. I work on setting boundaries each day. This is what works for me. There is no right or wrong way for parents to respond—decide for yourself. Trust your intuition.

There are a few things to be cautious about:

Don't give money. Clients have told me, and Jess agrees, that money is a trigger. It will take a while for your addicted loved one to learn to handle money and pay their bills and not use the money for drugs or alcohol or be responsible with money and credit card debt.

But whatever you and your family decide to do, you will learn what is comfortable and right for you. No one—not a professional or another family member—

can say what is right or wrong for one person or the other. Deciding one day to shop for food for your loved one, pay for the subway, get new clothes, or none of those things, you will do it and learn from it as I have. But ultimately we have to do what works for us as parents, and we are all in uniquely different situations, all dealing with addiction, relapse and recovery back to relapse, and hopefully a sustained recovery.

During my daughter's opioid addiction, recovery and relapse cycle, I let go of my fantasy that she was just like me. I also let go of the belief that I could be everything to her, both mother and father. Watching her intense struggle with addiction, including relapse, hospitalization and recovery, and back to relapse from the addicting opioids pain killers and heroin, I learned that my daughter has her own path, a journey where she is learning to live with the unchangeable fact that like her father, aunts and uncles and grandfather, she is addicted to substances and she has to find a way back to sanity. She is now embracing her higher power, the 12-step program and the overwhelming need for minute-to-minute prayer in order not to relapse. She is powerless over substance of any kind and I am powerless to control her life, no matter how much I love her. She can never have a drink or smoke a joint. Today she is eating healthy organic foods and turning her will over to something greater than herself. She is learning that only through the grace of her higher power can she recover. There is hope that she will move forward knowing that she can never experiment with anything, not one glass of wine, not one joint of marijuana, a hard concept for people to embrace.

I pray every day. "Dear God, protect my daughter and heal her addiction forever," I pray at the beginning of meditation, and then I close my eyes and relax into the comfort of the meditation process, reminding myself that there is no end to this addiction process and that I must focus on myself. Every day I meditate and pray for Jess's well-being, her safety, her health, and that she will be protected by her higher power.

Things are getting better, as they did for her father, who has been in recovery for forty years as of this writing. Many years ago he remarried and raised a new family with three children, one of them in Alcoholics Anonymous. Addiction is a disease. There is a hereditary component to it. Genetic vulnerability contributes to the risk of developing addiction. Twin and adoption studies show that about 40% to 60% of susceptibility to addiction is hereditary. But behavior plays a key role, especially when it comes to reinforcing a habit.

Jess's father is married to a woman who is in recovery. Things got better for my ex-husband Jim, as it did for Jess's uncles and aunts, all of whom recovered and have thriving businesses and relationships. It is a lifetime disease that can only go into remission. That's all, no cure—just remission.

I will never be able to totally understand why my daughter became an addict. But she did, and one day at a time, she is finding her way back to a new "normal" where she is working again and embracing the concept of a higher power of her understanding through the 12-step program. Perhaps she will get married and have an ongoing relationship with someone, have a family, a house and be able to hold on to money.

Her last relapse when she experienced the delirium and hit bottom, diagnosed with a psychotic break from reality, meant letting go of the dream—the loss of the job, of the chance to move up the career ladder, at least for now, accompanied by grief, loss and tears. Kirkbride was Jess's bottom.

After the last relapse I gave up hope, afraid I would

be let down again. Today, I am hopeful, and every day I pray that things continue on an upward path. I do so now with more detachment, surrender and understanding of the third step in the 12-step program, "Made a decision to turn our will and our lives over to the care of God as we understood him." In meetings, Al-Anon reminds us that a higher power is watching over us and is in charge. The 12 steps and the surrender they teach bring me comfort. As a mother raising a child alone, I believed I was my daughter's higher power. I was there to protect her and to keep her away from her father's alcohol and opioid addiction. One of the biggest lessons was that my daughter has her own path and she will be guided towards it and protected by a higher power of her understanding. Jess and I have similarities, but she is not *just like me*.

When I first attended Al-Anon meetings, still blaming myself for her addiction, I often ruminated over what life might have been like had I gone to Al-Anon and Jess to Alateen, a program for the children of family members with the disease of alcoholism, when her father went into recovery so many years ago. I was thirty-six and Jess was three years old at the time. At the time, addiction had nothing to do with me. Through the years, I have heard many stories, including stories of children attending Alateen (a program much like Al-Anon but for young people) who later in life struggled with the disease of addiction, reminding me that it is a family disease with a biological component. There are no guarantees.

Recently Jess asked me to read a passage in *The Alcoholics Anonymous Big Book*, entitled "The Doctor's Opinion" (xxiii). In it, William D. Silkworth MD writes: "All these, and many others, have one symptom in common; they cannot start drinking without developing the phenomenon of craving. This phenomenon, as we suggested, may be the manifestation of an allergy which differentiates these people, and sets them apart as a distinct entity."[11]

Although there are still debates over whether or not addiction is a disease or learned, there is no doubt in my mind that there is a hereditary component to the disease which makes some people more susceptible to addiction. The facts are: Substance use is mood altering and long-term use changes the way the brain operates, altering neurotransmitter release. There are many factors that can cause addiction and my daughter

---

11. Alcoholics Anonymous Big Book, "The Doctor's Opinion" (xxiii), William D. Silkworth MD

was susceptible to all of them, including a major factor, which is beginning to abuse substance at an early age (she was smoking marijuana at fourteen). Slowly the disease increased and became worse when she struggled with chronic pain and used doctor prescribed medications to ease the pain, eventually losing control.

"I am thankful to God for this lesson and that I am getting it now. Things are getting better. It's been a long journey for both of us," I tell Jess one day. She agrees. "I too feel closer to God, to my higher power, and now I want to carry the message and do the service work that I am called on to do," Jess says. "I have been resisting it for years. For so many years I have been running away from the fact that I have an addiction and that I can never ever have even a beer. I want to drink like a normal person but I cannot," Jess said, now more in touch with her higher power, the God of her understanding.

"I am bringing people to the meeting in Kensington," she said one day. "All I can do is open the door, invite them to the meeting I am going to, but they have to keep coming back. I have stepped through the door. I know I said this before but this time it's different. I have to do what the old-timers in the program say to do—work the 12 steps, not just step one where I am powerless, or Step 12, carrying the Message. Go to meetings and stay." Jess is on a good track, and as she works her recovery program, I feel reassured—but the focus has to remain on me and my recovery. I have to continue to work my Al-Anon program every day. And every day I renew the commitment to my recovery.

Chapter 31

A few nights ago I had a dream in which my daughter was smoking marijuana. I was horrified at her lapse in judgment. "You are rationalizing that you can smoke marijuana and not be heading for a relapse. In fact," I continued on in the dream, "You have already relapsed." In the morning I hesitated to tell my daughter about the dream, but decided that it was okay to share it, something we continued to do from childhood. To my surprise she said that at work, on break, some of the employees were out in the back alley smoking pot. She went on to say that she reached out to someone in the 12 Step Program and processed how uncomfortable that made her feel. Her sober friend said to her, "You could be on a mountain top and someone would be doing something that you don't like, whether it be smoking pot, doing harder drugs, or some errant behavior. You can't stop their behavior, you can only control your own."

Perhaps I was sensing something on an inner level of awareness picked up in the dream. But either way, it comes back to the fact that the focus must be on me. She was doing well, was holding a job before the pandemic, and not using drugs or drinking alcohol. I can only hope her abstinence continues, but there are no guarantees. Living with the uncertainty of addiction is the most difficult part of the process for family members involved with a loved one struggling with the disease of addiction. My advice is to keep the focus on yourself, sometimes one minute at a time. Use prayer and surrender, spiritual principles and make yourself available to the Al-Anon 12-step program or some other avenue to give you the support you need to live your life one day at a time. Take care of yourself. Spend time with yourself getting to know a new you, a less codependent you, one not totally involved in the activities of loved ones who are using, and pray and meditate every day.

After living with me for three years, my daughter is on a low dose of methadone, having decreased from 200 milligrams to 20 milligrams, which she maintains through the pandemic. Until the pandemic, she was going to the clinic every day participating in weekly therapy groups and working, her methadone decreasing. Now, as of this writing in 2020, she receives a 14-day supply of methadone that she takes home, and she speaks to her counselor by phone weekly. She recently lost her job and AA meetings are closed. She participates in them through the Zoom online communication technology. Our time together has been a gift, watching her slowly recover, our relationship healing everyday by the grace of God. We have healed our family relationships by practicing the first three steps in the 12-step program:

1: I am powerless.
2: I came to believe that a power Greater than myself could restore me to sanity.
3: I turned my will and my life over the care of God as I understood him.

With love and many blessings to all of the families who struggle with a loved one's addiction. Your friend, Raven Ruthe.

References and bibliography

(1) https://www.addictioncenter.com/news/2020/03/philly-opioid-strategies-kensington/

(2) https://www.drugabuse.gov/publications/research-reports/marijuana/what-are-marijuanas-long-term-effects-brain

(3) https://www.psychologytoday.com/us/blog/vitality/201404/the-neuroscience-giving#:~:text=While%20the%20brain%20is%20remarkably,cause%20a%20boost%20in%20mood.&text=Dopamine%20is%20connected%20to%20motivation%20and%20arousal.

(4) https://www.helpguide.org/harvard/how-addiction-hijacks-the-brain.htm

(5) https://www.cdc.gov/drugoverdose/data/statedeaths.html

(6) https://www.phoenixhouse.org/faq/what-happens-to-your-brain-when-you-take-drugs/

(7) https://drugpolicy.org/issues/drug-overdose

(8) https://drugpolicy.org/issues/drug-overdose

(9) https://www.hazeldenbettyford.org/articles/post-acute-withdrawal-syndrome

(10) https://www.samhsa.gov/medication-assisted-treatment/treatment/methadone

(11) Alcoholics Anonymous Big Book, "The Doctor's Opinion" (xxiii). In "The Doctor's Opinion," William D. Silkworth M.D

Contact:
RavenRuthe@gmail.com
Website: RavenRutheauthor.com

www.ingramcontent.com/pod-product-compliance
Lightning Source LLC
Chambersburg PA
CBHW022355040426
42450CB00005B/198